Anonymous Source

Anonymous Source

At War Against the Media
A True Story

Dan Cohen

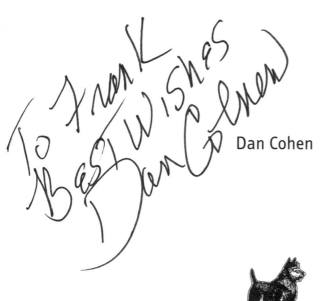

The Oliver Press, Inc.
Minneapolis

The Oliver Press, Inc.
Charlotte Square
5707 West 36th Street
Minneapolis, MN 55416-2510

Library of Congress Cataloging-in-Publication Data
Cohen, Dan, 1936-
Anonymous source: at war against the media; a true story/by Dan Cohen.
p. cm.
Includes index.
ISBN 1-881508-26-9
1. Cohen, Dan, 1936---trials, litigation, etc. 2. Cowles Media
Company--Trials, litigation, etc. 3. Confidential communications--Press--
Minnesota. 4. Estoppel--Minnesota. 5. Damages--Minnesota. I. Title

KF228.C633C64 2005
342.77608'53--dc22

2005042638

Printed in the United States of America

11 10 09 08 07 06 05   8 7 6 5 4 3 2 1

*To Elliot Rothenberg
and all the brave souls who
testified for me at the trial*

Hell hath no fury like a vested interest masquerading as a moral principle.

—Representative Barber Conable

I don't think we're the most widely-ridiculed paper in the country anymore.

—Doug Grow, columnist, *Minneapolis Star Tribune*, June 8, 2003

Meanwhile, the *Minneapolis Star Tribune*, probably the nation's most politically correct big-city daily, says it may drop its policy of censoring "offensive" names of sports teams.

—James Taranto, *Wall Street Journal*, June 4, 2003 (with thanks to *The Rake* for reminding all of us what a silly newspaper the *Star Tribune* is)

Contents

Foreword

Early in my career, while still attending college and covering a suburban beat for the *St. Paul Pioneer Press*, I learned the value of anonymous sources. While I was on my daily rounds, a judge cornered me and offered to tip me off to a good story—provided that I keep his name confidential.

His tip led to one of the best stories of my thirty-seven-year newspaper career. The judge told me that one of his colleagues—a probate judge in an adjoining county—was appointing his cronies to "appraise" large estates and awarding them huge fees. The work consisted mainly of signing their names to appraisals done by the trust companies administering the estates.

Recognizing that he had a rookie on his hands, my tipster not only pointed me toward the story, but instructed me on exactly how to check it out—what kinds of files to pull and where to look. For the next several months, I did just that and assembled a story showing that the probate judge was steering thousands of dollars in fees to his friends—including several prominent local officials. After the story appeared, state investigators swept in and established that the probate judge was not merely enriching a few of his fishing buddies. He was collecting sizable kickbacks.

The judge ultimately was convicted on criminal charges and removed from the bench, and state probate law was overhauled.

Anonymous sources are a vital tool for journalists. They help expose abuse of power, misuse of public funds, and plain old incompetence. But for every well-intended whistle-blower, there are at least as many politicians, government officials, and public relations practitioners who try to use the cloak of anonymity to plant rumors, discredit their political enemies, float trial balloons, and spin stories for their party's advantage.

Reporters want all of the news tips they can get, anonymous and otherwise. It's their job to check out the tips and decide which ones merit serious investigation. For every tip I received that resulted in a news story, I probably checked a dozen more that were inaccurate, inconsequential, or impossible to substantiate.

In *Anonymous Source*, Dan Cohen provides us with a case study in dumb mistakes by smart people. Cohen made the mistake of allowing himself to be used to leak a story in the final days of a political campaign about a petty crime that had been committed years earlier by an opposing candidate. Cohen tipped not just one reporter to the story, but four—greatly increasing the risk that he would be publicly implicated. Even if all four reporters and their news organizations had honored their pledge to keep Cohen's name confidential, it would not have taken a political genius to track the story to its source.

But Cohen was not the only actor in this political drama who made a mistake in judgment. Before accepting the material Cohen was offering, and promising to shield his identity, the four reporters needed to determine whether the information was worth having. A twelve-year-old shoplifting conviction hardly seems serious enough to disqualify someone from statewide office.

But the worst error in judgment was made by the editors of the St. Paul and Minneapolis newspapers. By identifying a source who had been promised confidentiality by their respective reporters, these editors undermined the integrity of their newspapers and discouraged would-be sources from coming forward with vital tips about stories their readers deserved to see.

If these editors thought the information provided by Cohen was inconsequential or irrelevant, all they had to do was discard it—as journalists do with tips every day. It is difficult to understand why the editors decided to name Cohen. He hardly was the first political operative to try to leak a story that would damage a candidate of the opposition party. It happens in virtually every election.

In the wake of the Cohen case, editors in Minnesota and around the country attempted to reduce the use of anonymous sources. Many insisted that reporters check with their supervisors before promising confidentiality to any would-be tipster. But such sources remain essential if news organizations are to perform their watchdog function—to expose waste and corruption, injustice and ineptitude.

Steven Dornfeld

The writer is a former political reporter, editor, and editorial writer who worked for both the *St. Paul Pioneer Press* and the *Minneapolis Tribune*.

Preface

Cohen v. Cowles Media, the case you will read about here, is a landmark of First Amendment law. It stands for the proposition that freedom of the press does not exempt the press from laws of general applicability. In other words, when journalists make a deal and break it, they are responsible for their actions, the same as ordinary mortals. It was a ruling that astonished and infuriated press lords long accustomed to doing whatever they pleased to whomever they pleased and has led to much weeping and wailing among their brethren.

The legal significance of the case has been the subject of countless articles and several books, but there isn't much discussion of that here. Even though I'm a lawyer, I never cared much about the legal issues. Neither did the defendants, the newspapers. Not that we didn't proclaim the sanctity of contracts, and not that they didn't raise their First Amendment privilege at every opportunity. Lawyers' talk. For those who are interested, a complete legal record of *Cohen v. Cowles Media,* 501 U.S. 663 (1991), can be found at the Harvard Law School Library.

For the litigants, the law here was the battlefield on which a human conflict was fought. Making legal history was a byproduct, not an objective. These pages do not dwell on the fine points of legal theory and disputations about who occupied the higher moral ground; rather, the focus here is on the *v.,* as in *versus.* This was not a pressed pants debate in the school auditorium. It was a switchblade fight under the stands.

For ten years, the Minneapolis and St. Paul dailies and I were locked in a battle that had little to do with Constitutional principles or money and had everything to do with strong mutual dislike—who could cause the greatest permanent damage and humiliation to the other side. The papers had no respect for me, then or now, nor I for them. And though the case is long since over, the beat goes on. Then and now, the *Minneapolis Star Tribune* swings the biggest cat in our flyover Midwestern town and malcontents are either ignored or stomped on.

Cohen is the story of the one time it didn't turn out that way. But not before I got off to a painfully shaky start. My original lawyer bailed out after I refused to accept a $4,000 "no apology" settlement. Expert witnesses trembled at the thought of antagonizing the keeping-score-forever papers.

I wound up with a lawyer much like myself, a Jewish Republican, a rare type anywhere, but especially so in heavily Scandinavian/German Minnesota. Though I had been elected to the Minneapolis City Council and he had been elected to the state legislature, where he served from 1978 to 1982, both of us had been defeated trying to climb the next rung of the political ladder. Like me, he was angry and embittered, and totally on his own, practicing law out of his home. Of much greater significance, and fortunately for me, he had the brains and the guts to take what was widely regarded as a hopeless case against the biggest bullies in the state. He located an equally gutsy and totally unlikely expert, the former editor of the local Catholic paper. This trim, dapper, charming, and erudite gentleman, who was probably pushing seventy, was the best witness to appear for either side at the trial.

The case took ten years from the day the suit was filed until it was all over. Not as long running as the case that passed from generation to generation in *The Pickwick Papers*, but long enough so that people would ask me how I felt about having to put up with the seeming endlessness and uncertainty of it all. Ten years is a long time to wait for closure to a life-changing event, particularly when the ultimate determination rests in the hands of people unknown and unapproachable except in the most formal settings. Who could know whether the judges might have ideological agendas of their own or simply seize on an oddball detail to make their decisions? Nonetheless, my answer has always been the same: I wish the case had lasted twenty years. It was thrilling to be on equal footing with my opponents—which is what the American judicial system in its wisdom and greatness not only promises, but delivers—and to have those arrogant bastards in our sights half the time, instead of always being in theirs. What made it all the more fun was that it was obvious they hated it every bit as much as I loved it.

It was not until years after the last court had rendered the last opinion that I decided to write this book. I couldn't do it until I had put the whole business far enough behind me to give it some perspective and balance and not just hammer out a revenge book. I had to face the fact that I was no knight in shining armor. The papers had not initiated the incident that started it all. I had made this mess wholly out of my own stupidity and ego-driven desire to be a player again in politics.

So while I have no trouble casting the papers in the villain's role in this melodrama, if there are heroes here, they are my lawyer, Elliot Rothenberg, and the American judicial system, which gave me as good a result as I could have hoped for, and in the judgment of some, better than I deserved.

CHAPTER ONE

Kentucky Fried Politics

Seven a.m., Tuesday, October 26, 1982, one week before the general election of November 2. I was on the tarmac of a small private airport outside St. Paul, Minnesota, waiting in a rented limo with a driver and a local newspaper columnist, Barbara Flanagan of the *Minneapolis Star Tribune*, the survivor of the *Minneapolis Star* and *Minneapolis Tribune* merger that had taken place that April. The governor of Kentucky, John Y. Brown, a foreshadower of the Bill Clinton school of public relations, was a hundred feet away in his plane deciding how long to diddle us before he made an appearance.

Meanwhile, the great mystery of the moment remained unsolved. Had John Y. brought his wife, Phyllis George, the former Miss America and better-known half of the marriage?

I thought he had. Barbara thought he hadn't, but she'd gotten up at five anyway to find out. Barbara didn't complain about it. She was so genuinely nice that she wrote a genuinely nice gossip column.

John Y. finally emerged. No Phyllis. Barbara asked John Y. a few perfunctory questions and melted away. The day had officially begun.

I was there as a PR guy, an employee of a local advertising agency, working that day on behalf of the Minnesota Thoroughbred Association. Kentucky's governor had come to Minnesota to promote the passage of a state constitutional amendment that would permit on-track pari-mutuel betting on horse racing. Raising and selling racehorses is big business in Kentucky and promoting the state's industries is one of the things governors do, though I doubt if many did it quite like John Y.

John Y. played it as a celebrity, not as your down-home, just-us-folks, next-door neighbor. At each appearance, the sea parts, the gov sweeps into the room, taking charge, lean and hungry aides trailing behind him. Think of lots of Stephanopouloses.

And so the day went, from press conference to editorial board meeting, to luncheon speech, to talk show appearance, to live television interview, to gubernatorial nap, to cocktail party, to the limo, and back to the tarmac.

John Y. didn't display his command presence for his meeting with the editorial boards of the local papers. Editorial writers are on top of the political food chain, even though working journalists sneer at them. They say that writing editorials is like wearing a blue serge suit and wetting your pants. It makes you feel warm all over and nobody notices. The truth is, everyone—everyone in the media—does notice. Editorial writers are the real spin doctors for their media brethren, and smart pols like John Y. know it. When captains of industry meet with the president of the United States, the president doesn't come to their offices, they come to his. When the president meets with the editorial board of the *New York Times*, he goes to the offices of the *New York Times*.

"You know about the eleven secret ingredients?" the governor confided to me on the way to the airport. He had made his fortune as the owner of Kentucky Fried Chicken. The current slogan had to do with the seasonings. "Well, 85 percent of them are salt and pepper."

Eighty-five percent. Who ever would have thought it? That's my dining-out story from my day with the legendary John Y. Brown.

I got home at about eleven that night. My wife, Gail, gave me a message. A colleague of mine, Gary Flakne, had called. There was to be a meeting of the Whitney campaign committee at eight the next morning. Be there.

CHAPTER TWO

City on a Hill

I had taken a roundabout route to the tarmac—lawyer, stockbroker, politician, in-house writer, PR guy—which had paved the way for me getting that call. Cops have a phrase for describing occupational nomads of my ilk: word dinks. The packaging may change from time to time, but the contents are always the same: alphabet soup.

After I graduated from college, I spent three years escaping real life by attending law school and two more years escaping the practice of law, for which I was profoundly unsuited. My next stop was as a speech writer/factotum for my father's partner, Wheelock Whitney. Like me, Whitney was also trying to make good his escape, in this case, from the securities business to the United States Senate. Whitney came from a wealthy St. Cloud family that had invested wisely in local utilities and farms, and was bored to the gills peddling stocks and bonds. Whitney's peers, Republicans George H.W. Bush and Peter Dominick, were also busy building political careers. Bush was running for the U. S. Senate in Texas, and lost to an incumbent Democrat, Ralph Yarborough, in the LBJ landslide. By that time, Dominick, who, like Whitney, had a background in the securities business, had already won a Senate seat in Colorado. Whitney picked 1964, the year of the Goldwater wipeout, to try it. It was a bad choice for a Republican. He was swamped by the Democratic incumbent, Eugene McCarthy.

As George Bernard Shaw said, "Every profession is a conspiracy against the laity." Working for Whitney, I learned a few tricks of the political trade. I decided to go into business for myself.

Shortly after the Whitney campaign for Senate closed down, the Cohen campaign for alderman opened up. I lived in a silk-stocking Republican ward, the Minneapolis equivalent of the old seventeenth congressional district in New York City that John Lindsay represented at the time.

Because municipal elections were officially nonpartisan, the general election consisted of the two top vote-getters in the primary, regardless of party. There were ten candidates. My Democratic opponent in the primary, Richard Windhorst, didn't make the ticket for the general.

I did and so did a former alderman, Romeo Riley. With a name like that, Romie probably would have been elected forever in a more ethnically diverse city than Minneapolis, but the Italian/Irish medley did no more for him than the name Cohen did for me in this predominantly Scandinavian/German city. Romie had been an alderman for more than twenty years. He also sold soap to many of the city's licensed bars and restaurants. Romie's sideline—with its potential for conflicts of interest—didn't meet the approval of the editorial writers at the Minneapolis papers, and ultimately, not of the voters, either. Romie's time had passed, and I won easily.

I was one of three youngish Republicans elected for the first time that year. Arne Carlson was another. Carlson and I became rivals for the next four years. After that, as I sunk beneath the waves politically, he held on, first as a legislator, then as state auditor, and eventually, as governor of Minnesota.

I had no particular ambition to participate in statewide politics. The city was my beat, and if the city hall environment was closer to *The Front Page* than it was to Ronald Reagan's City on a Hill, that suited me just fine. I'd get a call at home. I'd take my wife to a parking lot in the corner of an industrial park. That's where we did our big-ticket shopping. In the back of semis. By flashlight. I was once dumb enough to pay by check. The check wound up in the hands of a CPA. I have no idea how he got it, but he did, and I was subpoenaed when he was prosecuted for tax evasion. When I got to the federal courthouse, the area outside the courtroom looked like your average corridor at city hall: aldermen, vendors, clerks, secretaries, a big developer.

I said I lost the money in a poker game. So did everyone else. Actually, I did have a permanent seat at a weekly poker game at the home of the *Tribune's* city hall reporter, Pat McCarty. McCarty and the other newsies regarded city hall types with ill-concealed contempt. It wasn't only that McCarty skinned me every week at the poker table, and that the newsies always beat us in touch football, it was the chasm that lay between us in values, particularly between the newsies and the Republicans. They were idealists, irredeemably liberal, given to mocking us openly as they marched by us in civil rights parades. They regarded us as hacks, crooks, and cowards, and their mission in life was to expose our countless failings.

We saw them as self-righteous prigs, out of touch with the real world, protected in their jobs, unwilling to lay it on the line by running for what they believed in. They saw us as gutless. We saw them as gutless.

Being a Republican did have its advantages. Democrats had to show their labor credentials by having their campaign literature display a union bug, a tiny logo indicating the printing had been done at a union shop.

The guy who did our printing knew how to read the eensy-weensy numbers on the bug that showed exactly which printer had done the work. A couple of days before an election, when the candidates would be getting ready to unload their last-minute charges, he'd decode the bug and call the opposition's printer.

"I'm from the Democratic campaign," he'd say. "I can't make it down there tonight, but I need to proof that last piece you're printing for us. Can you read it to me over the phone?"

They did. Sometimes, we'd have our response out before the Democrats could even make their charges.

I served two two-year terms on the Minneapolis City Council. I ran the second time against token opposition, a magician named Pierre Vierete who said he "was going to make me disappear." It was a good line, but alas for Vierete, it only worked with rabbits. The Republicans retained their council majority. The incumbent Republican city council president, Glenn Olson, did not run for reelection as alderman, and in 1967 I was elected president of the city council.

In the same election, Democrat Arthur Naftalin was reelected to his fourth two-year term as mayor, narrowly defeating Arne Carlson, who, after only one two-year term on the council, had run a surprisingly strong race against Naftalin. One reason Carlson lost by only a handful of votes was that a bulwark of Naftalin's natural constituency, the editorial board of the *Minneapolis Tribune*, finally deserted him and endorsed Carlson, impressed by his youth and energy.

Naftalin had a long, distinguished career in local government and academics. He had been Hubert Humphrey's secretary when Humphrey was mayor. Humphrey is rightfully regarded as the best mayor Minneapolis ever had, so Naftalin came into office better prepared than anyone who had been mayor—including Humphrey. After Humphrey was elected to the Senate, Naftalin taught political science at the University of Minnesota, another great credential for the mayoralty.

Unfortunately, résumés do not a mayor make. Naftalin was cold, pompous, autocratic, an ideologue, and an intellectual snob incapable of the backslapping, wheeling-dealing style that greases the rails at city halls the world over.

Naftalin's milieu was the bow-tie crowd of academics, social workers, clergy, and assorted do-gooders. His mantra was charter reform. At home in the world of organization charts and new musty rules to replace old musty rules, Naftalin contended that the city charter granted too many powers to the council at the expense of the mayor. Why Minneapolis government would be less partisan and better managed if the mayor rather than the council were to appoint the city department heads was unclear, since they were all professional bureaucrats who hung on from one council to the next, decade after decade, regardless of which party was in power.

Still, it worked for Naftalin. It was the sort of shtick that his goo-goo constituency loved—until they got bored with it—and they were the opinion leaders who mattered in Minneapolis.

During this time, the summer of 1967, things were just beginning to heat up racially around the country. In the previous term, we had enacted new civil rights legislation, and Naftalin solicited suggestions from the new council for appointments to a commission on human relations.

I submitted the name of a white Democrat, a local lawyer and a classmate of mine at Harvard Law School, Michael Swirnoff. There was no acknowledgment. Naftalin submitted his fifteen choices to the council. There were six blacks on the list, including Ron Edwards, a car washer at the local gas utility. The next day a cop slipped me Edwards's rap sheet. He had served terms for, among other things, breach of the peace, and violation of the Huber Law, which allows workhouse inmates to hold jobs provided they return at night. He had recently been released from the workhouse after serving ninety days for wrongfully obtaining unemployment benefits. They were all misdemeanors. I, in turn, slipped the documents to a reporter, under cover of a promise of anonymity.

The story appeared on the front page of the *Tribune* on New Year's Day. Naftalin claimed he had been unaware of Edwards's record.

Naftalin and I had gone a few rounds already. Our most recent collision had involved an appointment to the Metropolitan Airports Commission (MAC), a plum slot because commissioners were able to cadge free airline tickets. Our first choice was Elsa Johnson, who had been defeated in the last election. Naftalin vetoed her, on the grounds that she was from the political community and therefore unworthy, a typically Naftalinesque formulation.

No one from the political community need apply? Well, let's see if he means it. Our next selection was Arne Carlson. Again, Naftalin vetoed, but he was beginning to look like a sore winner.

Our third choice was David Roe, the head of the building trades unions. Roe was another longtime Naftalin political rival. Naftalin had beaten Roe in a primary the first time he'd run for mayor. But Roe was a Democrat, and another veto would not only seem even more peevish than the last, but would also widen the split in the Democratic Party between intellectuals like Naftalin and blue-collar types like Roe. Naftalin swallowed hard, let Roe get the appointment unmolested, put another black mark in his grade book next to "Cohen," and waited for payback time. It wasn't long in coming. Ron Edwards was it. I had miscalculated badly. Though originally we had rejected Edwards's appointment by a ten-to-three vote, with three conservative Democrats joining a united Republican block of seven, my coalition was a lot shakier than it appeared.

First, the *Tribune* disclosed that I had been the one to give them Edwards's dossier, gratuitously breaking their promise of anonymity. I complained—privately—to the reporter whose byline appeared on the story linking me to the leak. He claimed the paper hadn't broken its word. He had figured it out for himself, and what did I care to do about it? Nothing? I was cowed. I knew I looked terrible. After all, if Edwards was such a poor appointment, why hadn't I simply disclosed his record up front and opposed the nomination? So I let it pass, and I stuck to attacking the appointee on his merits. What I should have done was ignore Edwards and slam Naftalin for sending down an appointment without vetting it properly. The people of Minneapolis were entitled to know, up front, why their mayor was proposing candidates with criminal records. Four years earlier, Naftalin had had to withdraw an appointment of a police chief when it was disclosed that he'd had several minor convictions. By concentrating on Edwards' record instead of Naftalin's, I had let it become a racial issue.

I had no particular animosity toward blacks, but I had no particular empathy for them, either. Before I got into politics, I never knew a black person by name. Every school I had ever attended, every neighborhood I had ever lived in, every outfit I had ever worked for, every social event I had ever attended was de facto segregated.

I hadn't noticed. And I hadn't cared. If blacks were being discriminated against, if they were at the bottom of the heap, that wasn't my fault. What was all the fuss about?

The editorial board of the Minneapolis paper provided that unwelcome enlightenment. Editorial thunderbolts rained down. We needed authentic types to represent voices that weren't being heard. Edwards's record was irrelevant; my opposition was mean-spirited.

Soon enough, the black community piled on, threatening to boycott the new commission and strangle the baby in its crib. The always-too-thin fabric of racial harmony was being ripped apart. Clergymen preached sermons. Numerous angry meetings took place.

Naftalin smelled blood—mine—and unhelpfully sent the appointment down a second time without bothering to consult us in advance, just as I had done with the MAC appointment. We vetoed it a second time, heating up the atmosphere even more.

While Naftalin and I were groveling in the tactical aspects of the case, better minds than ours had grasped its strategic significance. Despite its pretenses of sophistication, Minneapolis was still a backwater, held back by many of the same attitudes that had mired the South.

The Minneapolis Club, the place where the movers and shakers had lunch every day, did not admit Jews as members. Neither did the American Automobile Association. When I was a kid, my father had to join the Chicago AAA in order to get the maps and routing information for a family vacation. That sort of thing was penny-ante compared to what blacks had to endure. They were routinely denied admission not just to private clubs, but also to hotels, restaurants and, it goes without saying, decent employment. Politicians like Humphrey had been gradually bringing members of the business community to the realization that if Minneapolis were going to become a major corporate headquarters city, they would have to shake off their prejudices.

A few visionary businesspeople got with the program. Among them was John Cowles Jr., the relatively young publisher of what would become the *Minneapolis Star Tribune*, the son, heir, and namesake of John Cowles Sr., the founder of the *Tribune's* parent company, Cowles Media. The younger Cowles was a founder of the Minneapolis Urban Coalition, a newly formed coalition of Minneapolis business leaders and black community leadership.

Cowles had gotten off to a rocky start as a journalist. As a cub reporter, he had been assigned to cover the University of Minnesota, a not-too-strenuous beat. One morning, as Cowles went out to the garage behind his garden apartment, he noticed a pair of legs sticking out from the bushes across the alley. Cowles got into his car, drove off to the University, called in the location of the corpse to the police, and went about his duties at the "U."

Cowles's employer, the newspaper, found out about the matter somewhat later.

The body was that of Mary Moonen. She had been strangled and stuffed in the bushes by Dr. A. Arnold Axelrod. Dr. Axelrod was a married Jewish dentist and Mary's lover. In a sensational trial, Dr. Axelrod was convicted of manslaughter. (Ben Hecht, the coauthor of *The Front Page*, had reported a similar case in a story headlined "Dentist Fills Wrong Cavity.")

Seasoned reporters at the paper felt that Cowles's news sense was fatally fucked up. He not only had delayed calling in the story to the *Tribune's* news desk, but he had also called the cops before he had called the paper—exactly what a good citizen, but not a reporter, should do. Forever after, the old-time newsies called him "John John" or "Junior." Still, Cowles was decent, intelligent, and determined to use his considerable power to bring Minneapolis in line with the more progressive cities in the country. The Edwards case was the perfect catalyst, the Urban Coalition was the perfect vehicle, and I was the perfect target for their first attempt to make their bones by scoring a major civil rights victory.

By now, the mood in the city was getting ugly, and the business community was nervous. Cowles orchestrated the effort to reverse the city council's decision of vetoing Edwards. The big downtown retailers sent their suits over to city hall to set us straight. Racial problems could escalate into riots. Riots could result in very bad things happening. To the city. To me, if I expected their future support for higher office. Back down.

An open letter to me from Ray Plank, a prominent businessman and big-time Republican, appeared on the front page of the *Tribune*, the Cowles family newspaper. Same message, now delivered publicly, in even stronger terms. According to Plank, I was "playing with matches next to an open keg of dynamite."

Back down.

I was a coward. I did.

This time I was the one who swallowed hard. I asked Naftalin to submit the appointment a third time. It passed, with five votes from Republicans and three votes from Democrats.

"The council would rather be part of the solution than part of the problem," I said afterward. "Like the community itself, we may use this appointment as a tool to bring us closer together or as a wedge to drive us further apart. We may use it to go forward together or hang back divided. We have gone but an inch or a foot or a yard. The journey may take many miles." Noble thoughts. Did I really believe them? Had I learned anything other than the standard political fiddle of feigning enjoyment while eating a turd sandwich?

Not really.

And years later, in a nearly identical situation, I would give a repeat performance.

CHAPTER THREE

Will Work for Food

I ran for mayor of Minneapolis in 1969 and lost to a law-and-order candidate, Charlie Stenvig, a sergeant with the Minneapolis police department. 1969 saw the logical extension of the riots of the long, hot summers of '67 and '68. It was the year of the cop, not the year of the Cohen.

During the 1968 contest for the Republican nomination between Nelson Rockefeller and Richard Nixon, I had gone against the liberal grain of the Republican Establishment and been an early and ardent Nixon supporter. It wasn't called the Establishment for nothing. It was a closed circle. Had I supported Rockefeller, I would have been standing at the back of a long, long line of people with a lot more money, credentials, and time in service than me.

Nixon represented opportunity. I was the second elected public official in the state to openly endorse his candidacy.

Nixon also represented a real emotional commitment for me. I liked Nixon. He came from a hardscrabble background. As a young man, he had lousy athletic skills, yet was determined to play football, even if it meant being a human tackling dummy. He had none of the personal glamour and charm of pretty boys like Kennedy and Rockefeller—and none of the arrogance, either.

The first time I met him, during Whitney's campaign for the Senate, I realized he was so hirsute he actually had hair growing from the *top* of his nose. I liked that, too. He would not look down his hairy nose at city hall types like me. I wound up running an operation called Mayors for Nixon, which managed to raise a modest amount of money and generate some media attention.

I had a punch left on my Nixon chit, so after losing the mayoral election, I used it to go to Washington for a while as a PR guy in the Peace Corps. I hated it, was back to Minneapolis within six months, and ran for alderman again in my old ward. By this time, I was the Romeo Riley of my generation, soundly beaten by a younger, less shopworn candidate.

Years passed, and I drifted through a couple more jobs: stockbroker, in-house writer for a publishing firm, and finally a PR guy for an advertising agency, Martin/Williams. I wrote annual reports and brochures, helped with pitches to a couple of advertising accounts, and acted as an account exec on a couple of others. And, as usual, just when things seemed to be nailed down on my day job, I began messing around in politics again. I made my last try for elective office.

This time, it was the county board. The incumbent was a maverick woman Democrat, Nancy Olkon, who had won when her slogan, "She's Not Just One of the Boys," was still fresh. The Democrats endorsed a strikingly handsome young legislative aide named Mark Andrew to oppose her in a bitter internecine fight. Though a vote analysis showed the district to be 53–47 Democratic, if Olkon and Andrew split the Democratic vote in the nonpartisan primary, I might be able to sneak onto the general election ticket and possibly pick up the support of the losing Democrat.

It was an issueless campaign for me. My secret motto was "Why don't you and him fight?" I just wanted to get out enough Republicans for the primary so I could make it to the general election Unfortunately for me, the Olkon/Andrew split energized the Democrats for the primary, while my dull campaign energized no one. The whole thing was mercifully brief, and by mid-September it was over.

That's when I got a call to work on the 1982 Whitney campaign for governor.

CHAPTER FOUR

The Race for Governor

While I had been puttering around in the bush leagues of politics, Whitney had been preparing for another shot at the majors. This time, running for governor, he positioned himself to avoid the Republican Party insider tag he had worn when he ran against McCarthy in 1964. He was also pro-choice, while the delegates to the Republican endorsing convention were strongly anti-abortion. Whitney didn't seek the Republican endorsement. Instead, he ran in the primary against the convention-endorsed Republican candidate.

Whitney hired the hot new agency in town, Fallon McElligott, to do his advertising. They produced a series of clever television spots featuring exploding piggy banks, shooting galleries, and windup dolls, and Whitney had the money to run them frequently. He won the primary easily and became the official Republican choice for governor.

His Democratic opponent in the general election was Rudy Perpich. Perpich was a former lieutenant governor who had become governor in 1976 when his predecessor, Wendell Anderson, arranged to have himself appointed to the United States Senate to succeed Walter Mondale, who had resigned to serve as Jimmy Carter's vice president. Perpich was swept out of office along with the overreaching Anderson in 1978.

Perpich was the son of Croatian immigrants, who had come in large numbers to work in Minnesota's Iron Range area under brutal conditions at the turn of the century. He entered the first grade unable to speak English. Determined to make something of himself, Perpich graduated from the University of Minnesota dental school and went back to the Iron Range to practice dentistry. He was later elected to his local school board and then to the state senate. There, he became a powerful voice for the northeastern corner of the state, which had a chronically distressed economy and was overwhelmingly Democratic.

Like Whitney, Perpich had bucked his party's official ticket in 1982 and in the primary had beaten the endorsed candidate, Attorney General Warren Spannaus. Perpich had run a strong populist campaign and had the overwhelming support of his loyal Iron Range constituency. Years earlier, Perpich, as a candidate for lieutenant governor, had successfully used his northern Minnesota/Catholic/Eastern European background to balance Wendell Anderson's Twin Cities/Lutheran/Scandinavian appeal. Leading the ticket was something else.

But then, Whitney was hardly cut from the standard Minnesota model for governors either, with his Yankee name and preppy background.

Minnesotans select the governor and lieutenant governor as a team. Because both Whitney and Perpich had avoided the convention process, they were able to make personal selections for the lieutenant governor slot relatively free from any constraints. Both candidates had chosen outsider lieutenant governor candidates for their outsider tickets. Whitney's choice was Lauris Krenik, a University of Minnesota regent and small-town farmer unknown outside Republican Party circles.

Perpich's running mate, Marlene Johnson, like Krenik, had never run for public office, but she was a far more politically inspired choice. For one thing, she was the only Scandinavian on either ticket. For another, in an era when women were becoming increasingly aware of their political muscle and eager to use it, she was the first woman to be the official choice of either party for lieutenant governor. Not the least of her assets was that she ran an advertising agency, and presumably her deal with Perpich included attractive terms for what had become every campaign's single largest expense.

My work for Whitney had consisted largely of writing a couple of position papers, one on agriculture and another on a program he called the Minnesota Enterprise Fund. After the primary, I'd also appeared as a Whitney spokesperson on a panel on the local public television station, where we were questioned by the local press, including Lori Sturdevant, the *Tribune* reporter assigned to the gubernatorial campaign.

Fallon McElligott shot a new set of commercials for the general election. I spent a morning standing around a TV studio shouting nasty questions off-camera at Whitney while he responded "spontaneously." I think the idea was to replicate the man-in-the-arena spirit of the old 1968 Nixon infomercials, but these talking head spots didn't work nearly as well as Whitney's preprimary ads.

Fallon McElligott sent me a check for $500, made out to me personally, for my work on the TV spots. Freelancing on outside accounts is a way of life in the advertising business. Agencies tolerate it, because by letting their employees earn outside income, the agencies are better able to underpay them. I could have treated the account as a freelance, but I didn't. I endorsed the check over to Martin/Williams. The Whitney campaign was to be a house account.

Gary Flakne, an old political buddy and member of Whitney's brain trust, called my house during the day I had spent with John Y. Brown. It was a week before the general election, and Whitney was trailing in his own polls by twenty points. As usual, I was on the prowl for anything that would enable me to log a few more hours on the old time sheet.

"So where's the meeting?" I asked my wife, Gail, who had taken the message—this being the prehistoric era before the invention of the cell phone.

"Whitney headquarters," she said.

CHAPTER FIVE

Fawked

I was so far out of the loop that I thought the Whitney campaign headquarters were located at the family business office downtown. My car was being repaired, as usual, and the next morning Gail let me off at the Dain Tower offices of the Whitney Land Company. Bemused by this would-be political strategist who couldn't even find the campaign office, staffers at the Whitney Land office set me straight and I took a cab to the right location.

The Whitney campaign headquarters were on the edge of downtown in the Fawkes Building, a ramshackle, low-rent, three-story office building owned by Whitney's wife, Irene. I knew the Fawkes Building well. It never should have been built; it was sinking into a bog and on the verge of falling down. When I had been a member of the city planning commission, the previous owners had besieged us for relief from the countless orders issued by city building inspectors to bring the building up to code. We, in our passion for preserving the pristine character of this historically significant pile, repeatedly refused. "You've been Fawked," was the order of the day. The owners found another solution: pass on the problem to a new sucker.

The meeting was held in an airless chamber on the second floor. I had to take the stairs because the elevator never worked; the building was slanted like the Leaning Tower of Pisa, and the elevator kept getting stuck in its shaft.

There were five of us there: Arnold Ismach, a professor of journalism at the University of Minnesota and Whitney's media consultant; Jerry Olson, director of government affairs at Pillsbury and a former professional Republican field man; George Thiss, an aide to United States Senator David Durenberger and a former chair of the Minnesota Republican Party; Gary Flakne, a lawyer and former state legislator and Hennepin County attorney; and me. Except for Ismach, I had known everyone at the meeting for at least twenty years. Thiss had been my counselor at summer camp in northern Minnesota. He had made me share my comic books with my fellow campers. I was six years old at the time.

Flakne chaired the meeting. He reported that on Tuesday, a local call-in radio talk-show host named Dick Pomerantz had scheduled a joint appearance between our tiger, Lauris Krenik, and Marlene Johnson. Johnson was a no-show. Pomerantz had asked Krenik, "Suppose there was something in somebody's background twelve or fifteen years ago, a petty theft. Should that person be judged on that?" While Pomerantz didn't mention Johnson specifically, Krenik left the studio with the impression that the reference was to her.

Krenik called Whitney's campaign manager, Jann Olsten, who called Flakne and asked him to check it out. Flakne went to the St. Paul court archives, where he found that a Marlene Marie Johnson had two arrests on her record. He had made copies and passed them out to us at the meeting. In September 1969 she had been arrested for unlawful assembly in what appeared to be a civil rights protest over the city's failure to hire minority workers. The charges were dismissed in April 1970.

The second arrest came on May 25, 1970. She was arrested in a Sears store a few blocks from the state capitol for petit theft. There was no indication of what property was involved. The next entry showed that on June 3, she pled not guilty and was convicted in a trial held before a judge. The judge deferred sentencing until February 6, 1971, at which time the charges were dismissed and the conviction vacated. He also referred her to a doctor.

Obviously, we weren't going to make an issue out of a civil rights protest.

The petty theft was probably shoplifting. Vacating the charges after a few months from the time of the theft was common in first-offense shoplifting cases. The doctor part was also standard practice. The idea was the doctor would help her understand why she did it.

Now what would we do with it? There wasn't much enthusiasm for doing anything. Nobody knew much about Johnson. We weren't even sure this Marlene Marie Johnson was the same person who was running for lieutenant governor. As for the offense itself, it wouldn't have been terribly shocking if the doer had been the mayor of Minneapolis. It was a desultory meeting. We were peeved that the story hadn't come out sooner and convinced that the mainstream press knew about it—thousands of people listened to Pomerantz's show—and they simply hadn't reported it because of a pervasive cultural bias against speaking ill of any Democrat. The more probable—and less paranoid—explanation was that they did know about it but didn't report it because they regarded it as too trivial.

"You know, two years ago I got arrested in Louisville," I said, going into my storytelling mode, "at the Kentucky Derby. I had two extra tickets. I went over to the clubhouse area where all the scalpers hang around, and I held up my tickets and said, 'I am now going to conduct an auction.' A little group gathered around, and one guy said, 'I'll offer you face value.'

"'Face value? Are you nuts?'

"'No,' he said. 'You are.'

"He arrested me. He grabbed the extra tickets out of my hand. Then he made me turn my pockets inside out and give up my other ticket, the one I was going to use to get myself in. He hauled me over to a little hoosegow behind some hedges. It was a long truck trailer, divided lengthwise down the middle, with a row of floor-to-ceiling bars down one side and a counter for paperwork down the other. He stuck me behind the bars with a bunch of other clowns, and then he elaborately turned his back on me and began doing the paperwork.

"Well, I got it. The idea was, 'Take a walk, Dan.' You won't go to jail so long as you leave your tickets behind for the cops to sell. So I did. I walked out of the cell and out the door. Escaped. Just like Willie Sutton. Only now, I didn't have a ticket to the Derby. So, genius that I am, I walked back over to the same area where I'd been arrested, and this time I tried to *buy* a ticket from a scalper. Nothing illegal about that, is there?

"Maybe not, and maybe it just pissed off the cop who'd arrested me the first time, because he arrested me again and this time he locked the cell door.

"I got hauled down to the Jefferson County Jail in a paddy wagon with a bunch of other guys. We got fingerprinted, mug shot, strip-searched, thrown into a holding cell, brought before a judge, pled nolo, and got released. Thanks to a buddy who'd been waiting for me in the grandstand area with a live ticket, I was back at Churchill Downs in time to see the Derby.

"The story has a moral. I wrote about the whole thing in a column in the *Star* before I ran for county commissioner. Cleared the decks. That's what Marlene should have done. Come clean. Fessed up. Nobody would have cared. Instead, she concealed it. It isn't the shoplifting that's so terrible. It's not telling the voters about it."

By this time, I'd gotten myself all worked up.

"I'll carry the mail," I said, offering to take this bit of evidence to the press. "But if I'm going to do it, I'm going to do it as an anonymous source." Fateful words.

CHAPTER SIX

Anonymous Source

Despite the Edwards debacle years earlier, I'd been an anonymous source many times over the years, as recently as three weeks before the Marlene Johnson incident. During the same election cycle that Perpich and Johnson were running against Whitney and Krenik, Minnesotans were also electing a United States senator. The incumbent Republican, David Durenberger, was facing the department store heir, Mark Dayton, a Democrat.

One fine day in October, Dayton canceled a public appearance at the University of Minnesota and quietly slipped into Washington to meet with officials of the National Rifle Association. The NRA had been circulating rumors about some alleged Dayton antigun conduct, and he wanted to assure them that the rumors were false.

Unfortunately for Dayton, the whole thing may have been a setup to draw him into that meeting. After it was held, a pro-Durenberger NRA lobbyist contacted me. I had done some work for the NRA and I made a standard anonymous source arrangement with Betty Wilson, the *Star Tribune* reporter who was covering the Senate race. The spin on the story that ran on the front page of the *Star Tribune* was that Dayton, widely perceived as an orthodox liberal, was supping with the devil, trying to make deals with the NRA. Dayton lost the Big Mo and spent the next two weeks on the defensive until the story died down.

I had been around the block often enough to know that a liberal press would view a meeting with the NRA as a more serious offense than a criminal conviction for theft. At our Fawkes Building meeting, I asked Ismach how to handle the arrangements with the media regarding the Johnson incident. No harm in getting the journalism prof to coach me on how to do this by the numbers. I wanted no misunderstandings. I didn't care to get burned again like I had with Edwards.

Ismach drew up a media list for the Johnson story. There were three names: Lori Sturdevant of the *Minneapolis Star Tribune*; Bill Salisbury of the *St. Paul Pioneer Press*, the morning St. Paul paper; and Gerry Nelson of the Associated Press. I added a fourth name, Dave Nimmer, a reporter at WCCO television. In his last post at the *Star*, Nimmer had been managing editor. Sturdevant, Salisbury, and Nelson all had warrens in a press row in the basement of the state capitol in St. Paul. Nimmer worked out of the television studio in downtown Minneapolis.

Ismach suggested I call them beforehand and gave me a little litany to go through on the phone. I reached Sturdevant first.

"Are you going to be there this morning?" I said.

"Yes."

"I have information which may or may not pertain to the upcoming statewide election. If we can reach an agreement on the terms on which I'll give it to you, then I'll give it to you. I'd like to come over and discuss it with you."

She said fine. I made the same deal with Salisbury. When I tried Nelson, his line was busy.

I reached Nimmer. He was on his way out the door at WCCO to cover a murder trial in Minneapolis. I gave him the same pitch. We agreed to meet for lunch at a downtown deli.

Because I was sans car, Flakne chauffeured me to the suburban dealership where I recovered my '78 Pacer—not the classiest of spy mobiles for a big-time anonymous source.

I stumbled around the capitol basement until I found the press row. The offices were side by side, with little name signs jutting out from the door frames identifying the media outfit of each occupant.

I started with the *Star Tribune*. Sturdevant was alone at her desk.

"I have some materials here which may be of interest to you concerning a person who may be a candidate for statewide office," I said, sounding like the legal nerd I had spent the last twenty years trying not to be. "I will be happy to give you these materials assuming that we can reach an agreement. And the terms of the agreement would be that you would promise me confidentiality; that my name would not be used in the article; that I would be given anonymity and you would not pursue me with my source of having received these materials. If you give me that promise, I, in turn, will give you these materials and go over them with you."

She agreed.

I handed her a copy of the documents, and we briefly discussed the contents. I carefully avoided any personal characterization or accusations regarding Johnson. I had one hand on the doorknob when she asked me, "Do I have this exclusively?"

"No," I said. A small frown crossed her face.

"Come by any time you have material like this," she said, brightening.

Salisbury's office was just across the hallway. Another reporter, Bob O'Keefe, was on the phone. I wanted some privacy, so I asked Salisbury if we could get a cup of coffee. We went to the cafeteria where we sat at a table semi-hidden behind an arch in an alcove set apart from the main seating area.

I went through the same drill as I had with Sturdevant. He agreed. He went through the documents, looked up at me, and said, "This is political dynamite." End of conversation. No questions about exclusivity.

Next stop, Gerry Nelson of the AP.

His office was at the end of the hallway. We went back to the cafeteria and made the same deal. No comments. No questions.

That did it for the capitol press corps. I went back to my office, wound up some work in connection with John Y.'s visit the day before, and went to meet Nimmer for lunch.

I knew him much better than the other three, and I didn't put the proposition to him in the legalese I had used with them. After he scanned the documents, he said, "This stuff has been kicking around a couple of days."

Surprise.

I told him he didn't have it exclusively. He didn't seem to care.

By the time I got back to the office, clouds had begun to gather. Flakne called. Sturdevant had contacted him. She had been in touch with the document section of the St. Paul courts and had been able to identify him as the person who had signed for the documents relating to Johnson. It looked like the *Star Tribune* was trying to come in through the back door on our deal in order to find a way to identify the Whitney campaign as the source of the revelations about Johnson.

I was concerned for my client, Whitney, but as long as Flakne stonewalled as to my identity, it seemed to me the *Star Tribune* would have to honor our agreement.

I wandered out into the hallway outside my office and there was Dave Floren, my boss at Martin/Williams. I hadn't spent a lifetime in politics without having some idea of how to cover my backside. I told him what had happened, and that I anticipated there would be an article in the paper about it in which the Whitney campaign might be mentioned, but that I didn't think either Martin/Williams or I would be identified. His response was a nonresponse. He'd been around long enough, too, to realize what I was up to, and he wasn't about to give me a free pass until he knew how the whole thing would come down.

More calls. They didn't get any better. Nimmer told me that the press had questioned Johnson, and she said that the incident had taken place a month after her father's death, when she had been distraught. She had "forgot" to pay for a six-dollar sewing kit and was arrested. Six dollars. Six measly dollars. She had told Perpich about it before he named her as his running mate, and he had said it was irrelevant.

The next call was from Ismach. Salisbury had talked to Whitney's campaign manager, Jann Olsten, and indicated that he was going to be calling me later in the day to renege on his promise to me. That was the first hard indication I had that my deal was unraveling.

By the time I got home, Salisbury had called. I called him back. His first words were, "We're in trouble."

"How's that, Mr. Salisbury?"

"My editor, David Hall, told me I shouldn't have made a promise to you as I did, and we are going to renege on that promise, and we are going to run your name in connection with this matter," he said.

I was ready to do battle.

"Other reporters have gone to jail rather than reveal their sources," I said. "In the used-car business they retrade deals, but in the journalism profession they don't. We had an agreement. And I will expect you to honor that or not run the article."

Salisbury then asked me for permission to use my name. "Absolutely not," I said. "I am not letting you off the hook."

He was uncomfortable and apologetic and in almost as much distress as I was.

Next call. Lori Sturdevant. She had been talking to Salisbury. She told me if the St. Paul paper ran my name, the Minneapolis paper would, too.

"Because someone else breaks their word to me does not give you the right to break your word to me," I said. I did my used-car/journalists-behind-bars number on her, too, and added, "Nobody's threatening to send you to jail, and you people not only give me up, you lie to me."

"That's why I won't have my name on this article," she said. "I told them I can't do that. That is wrong."

"That is cold comfort, but some comfort," I said.

And that was that. There were various calls back and forth for the next couple of hours, but no movement. Finally, I said to Sturdevant, "You definitely are going to run this? Use my name? The whole works?"

"Yes, yes, yes. We are going to use it."

There was nothing left to do but try and make the best of it. Spin time.

"In that case, knowing you are going to run this and that all my arguments have failed and you have broken your word to me, I have something to say."

I gave Sturdevant a statement to the effect that it was not the offense that mattered, it was the concealment that was significant. "Every day Perpich and Johnson failed to reveal it to the public, they were living a lie," I said.

"What a nice statement," she said.

"A nice statement was not exactly what I had in mind making."

My long nightmare had begun.

CHAPTER SEVEN

Betrayed

I couldn't sleep. At two a.m. on Thursday, October 28, I began prowling the streets for the morning papers. The *Star Tribune* had not yet been delivered to the neighborhood drop points. I went downtown and snatched a copy from the loading dock. I had to drive to St. Paul to find a *Pioneer Press*.

When I got back home, I called Flakne. By this time, it was three a.m. I didn't care. I veered wildly between despair and bravado as I read the articles to him over the phone.

The front-page headline in the *Star Tribune* read, "Marlene Johnson arrests disclosed by Whitney ally." The byline was Staff Writer. Sturdevant had told me the truth. She had refused to let her name be used. It was her editors, Mike Finney and Frank Wright, who had broken the newspaper's word to me.

It was the same story in St. Paul, where the editor, David Hall, who later justified his decision by describing my conduct as "sleazy," ordered Salisbury to name me in his article.

For all Hall's repugnance, the St. Paul paper was much more cautious in its coverage. The *Pioneer Press* didn't put the story on the front page. They ran it on the first page of the D section, Metro/Region news, under the headline "Perpich running mate arrested in petty theft case in '70." It didn't mention my name until the thirteenth paragraph, although the source was identified as a "prominent Independent Republican" in the third paragraph.

Unlike the *Pioneer Press*, the *Star Tribune* article, true to its headline, had played up my role big time. The opening sentence read,

> Court records showing that DFL lieutenant governor candidate Marlene Johnson was convicted more than 12 years ago on a misdemeanor charge of shoplifting were given to reporters Wednesday by Dan Cohen, a friend and political associate of IR gubernatorial candidate Wheelock Whitney.

Whitney and Olsten sawed off the limb behind me, saying that I "had acted without knowledge or permission of the candidate or his staff." Olsten said that "as of yesterday afternoon"— hours after I'd met with the reporters—"the Whitney campaign had no plans to mention Johnson's record." Olsten, who had told Flakne about the charges, added, "I don't know how Cohen got the information about Johnson—he must have looked it up in the records." Flakne said he "could not say who gave him the information, or why he waited until this week to obtain copies of the documents."

Perpich's campaign manager accused Whitney of "eleventh-hour muckraking" and "desperation tactics." Head shots of Johnson and of me ran side by side on the jump page.

Johnson's version of what happened played prominently in both papers. According to the *Pioneer Press* article:

> Johnson said the incident occurred at a time when she was distraught over the recent death of her father. She said that on May 25, 1970, she walked out of the Sears store, 425 Rice Street, with *$6 worth of buttons and other sewing material* without paying for it (italics added). She was arrested.

> "I was very close to my father and was upset by his death," she said. "I was under stress—I had lost about 20 pounds—and I got my first speeding ticket at about the same time."

The Minneapolis version was similar, except for one thing. There Johnson's quote read:

> "I wasn't myself for quite a while. Within a month, I lost 20 pounds. I got my first-ever speeding ticket and, *when I forgot to pay for $6 worth of sewing materials* at the Sears store on Rice St., I was arrested" (italics added).

Well, which was it? Was she so grief stricken that her normal standards of conduct were impaired, or was she simply forgetful? No one ever bothered to question the seeming inconsistency between the two explanations. Okay, maybe she "forgot" to pay for the "$6 worth of sewing materials." That's the Minneapolis version. But in the St. Paul version, where the forgot explanation does not appear, she describes the articles as "$6 worth of buttons and other sewing material." In other words, at least two separate items. Are we supposed to believe she forgot to pay for not just one, but two things? And what evidence was there, other than what Johnson told the press, that the items taken were sewing materials with a value of only six dollars?

No matter. No one who supported her cared that a certified public record showed that she had been arrested for theft, pled not guilty, been tried according to law, been disbelieved by a judge and convicted of a crime. No one cared if or what she had stolen, whether she had concealed the conviction or was lying about it even now. No one cared that I had told the truth.

It was enough that Marlene Johnson, the first of her sex to be chosen for the honor of running for lieutenant governor, was being harassed by a seedy old pol over a minor incident that had taken place twelve years earlier when she was a mere twenty-four years old. The same day the story broke, a Perpich/Johnson campaign ad appeared in the *Pioneer Press*. The headline, which ran over a photo of Johnson and a lengthy supporter list, read, "When a woman does something that women have never done before, it changes us." There could be no doubt about what she and her supporters felt she represented, nor how they felt about any challenge to that presumption. What threatened her, threatened them.

I had trashed the candidate who, according to the newspaper ad, "understands the concerns of women and minorities in a way that no other candidate could." When Johnson defended herself, it was with arguments that exposed her as weak, vulnerable, emotional, and possibly even deceitful, the stereotypical negative feminine qualities that her candidacy was to have shown that women could transcend.

It made her all the more appealing to her supporters. She had been nominated because she was a woman. She was entitled to election because she was a woman. She had been criticized because she was a woman. She had responded to that criticism as a woman responds.

While I was shouting that the empress had no clothes, the spectators were shouting back that they loved her all the more for it. Now she was not just the first woman candidate. She was a martyred woman candidate.

Johnson was never questioned about the incident beyond what appeared in these two articles. No reporter ever interviewed her about it again. She was never deposed. She never testified under oath. She was never cross-examined. Though she was the linchpin around which the whole episode revolved, her role had ended. She vanished from sight, like a first-act murder victim. The rest of the show would be the whodunit.

CHAPTER EIGHT

Tarred, Feathered, and Fired

The *Star Tribune* article ran thirty-three paragraphs. For all its length and thoroughness, the story did not discuss the promise the paper had made to me and broken, nor did it offer any explanation as to why there was no reporter's byline. The *Pioneer Press* story took the disingenuous route, saying that Cohen "gave the court records to at least three reporters, but asked that his name not be used." No mention was made that I had been promised that it wouldn't be.

Nimmer's television station, WCCO-TV, hadn't used the story at all. Though the *Star Tribune* had deemed it to be front-page stuff, Nimmer didn't regard it as sufficiently newsworthy for even the briefest discussion.

Nelson also kept his word to me. The AP story, which was used on several radio and TV newscasts Wednesday evening, said court documents "were slipped to reporters," but didn't use my name.

Thursday was a day from hell. At Martin/Williams eyes were averted. Those that weren't held cold stares. There was a note in my in-box from a strong Democrat giving me a workout for having done this terrible thing to this wonderful woman.

My boss, Dave Floren, stopped by my office. He had his war face on. He said, "Be prepared for a meeting after lunch. Until then, consider yourself under suspension."

About fifteen minutes before the scheduled time for the meeting, Floren's boss, Don Haag, summoned me into his office.

He was mightily displeased. Our major client was Archer Daniels Midland, a company with a long history of political involvement. Haag could be expected to feel that my behavior would make Martin/Williams seem clumsy and amateurish to the sophisticated operatives at ADM. Haag put it on a moral basis. He said I had displayed a lack of character and a lack of judgment.

I tried to tough it out. I said I thought he may have been right so far as the lack of judgment was concerned because I had trusted people who betrayed me. As for the lack of character, I disagreed. I had told the truth. The record I gave the press was a true, valid copy of a public document that anyone could have obtained, and had the press been doing their job, they would have obtained it long before I did. The decision to give it to them was reached by five of us who felt we were acting appropriately because the opposing campaign had not come clean with the people of Minnesota. "It's like Watergate," Haag said.

"Yeah, I said, "but on the other side. They're the ones that had the criminal offense they didn't want the people to know about. We're the ones that told the truth." Haag said that if he had been at the meeting, he would have decided it differently.

"Well, here we were, an aide to a United States senator from Minnesota, a professor of journalism at the University of Minnesota, an executive at Pillsbury, a former Hennepin County attorney, and me, and we reached an agreement. You may have been able to persuade us otherwise had you been there, but this was not a group off the street. This was a fairly high-powered group." I was just making him angrier. Haag tried a new tack.

He said that advertising was a collaborative business, that it was dependent upon interpersonal relationships between members of the firm, and that I had destroyed all those relationships.

"Okay, some people are unhappy at the moment, but it's repairable," I said.

"No, it's not," said Haag, the unhappiest person of all. "It's terminal. You have made it impossible for you to continue here. There is nobody here who will work with you."

"I don't believe that's the case. I think it will blow over."

"NO. That *is* the case."

"Are you telling me that I have no choice but to resign?"

"That's what I'm telling you."

End of conversation. By this time, Floren had drifted into the office and was sitting behind me, while I faced Haag across his desk. I got up and went back to my office.

Floren told me Haag wanted me out of there that very day. Just out. I negotiated one more day on the basis that I simply couldn't tie up all the loose ends in a matter of a couple of hours.

The news, of course, was all over the shop in a matter of minutes and people drifted in and out of my office for the rest of that day and the next. I met with Floren again on Friday to work out a severance package.

Friday afternoon those few of my now-ex-associates who dared to be seen in public with me gave me what amounted to a farewell party in the saloon downstairs from our offices. So far as Martin/Williams was concerned, I was history.

So far as the rest of the agencies in town were concerned, I was poison.

Meanwhile, the drumbeat in the *Star Tribune* grew louder.

In Friday's paper, columnist Jim Klobuchar didn't much care for the "living a lie" statement I had given to Sturdevant.

I was a poseur, the self-appointed, self-righteous Conscience of the Community.

> Didn't Dan Cohen come clean with the world, he asks, when he got arrested for scalping tickets at the Kentucky Derby? ... Let's take this as a criterion for honesty—as enunciated by the hardball-playing publicist trying to get his candidate elected.

> Every candidate who withholds any information from the vot-
> ers that might bear on his or her character or integrity, profes-
> sionally or personally, is living a lie. That means all candidates on
> the ballot must come forward today with every marital indiscre-
> tion or act of adultery, every instance when they dragged on a
> joint of pot or worse at a private party, or got blasted out of their
> skulls on booze and howled racial epithets and profanity.

In the years since Klobuchar wrote the article, his exaggerat-
ed vision of peephole political culture is close to becoming real-
ity, thanks in no small part to the members of his own profession.

On Saturday, October 30, the day before Halloween, the *Star
Tribune* editorial page ran a not terribly original reprise of the
famous Herblock cartoon showing Nixon emerging from the
sewer. The *Star Tribune* version showed Rudy Perpich standing in
the doorway of his campaign headquarters on Halloween eve.
Several trick-or-treaters cavorted in the background. Perpich was
looking at a battered garbage can that had materialized on the
doorstep. Written on the garbage can were the words "Last
Minute Campaign Smears." A pair of eyes were peering out from
under the lid and a pair of feet protruded from the bottom of the
garbage can.

Perpich addressed the garbage can and said, "It's Dan Cohen."
On Sunday, a letter to the editor read:

> The release of information regarding Marlene Johnson's mistak-
> en exit of a store with unpaid sewing items, 12 years ago, is the
> absolute bottom of the barrel. The scraping of the barrel [is] that
> Wheelock Whitney considered this important information for
> the public.

> How many of us have at least once in our lives found ourselves
> mistakenly walking towards a store exit with merchandise in
> hand? It is startling when it happens. But it does happen.
> Incidents like this are even more prevalent in times of grief or
> major change. Johnson's later endeavors, whether personal, pro-

fessional or political should be allowed every success without regard to this incident.

—Helen M. Yates, Richfield

Unsurprisingly, Helen M. Yates had signed the Perpich/Johnson ad that had appeared in the *Pioneer Press* on Thursday. She was also a legislative candidate that year. Readers were not made aware of either her participation in Johnson's campaign or her candidacy. On Monday, the day before the election, there was another front-page article in the *Star Tribune*. The headline read, "Cohen quits job after election incident." The article went on to quote Floren as saying Cohen "had offered his resignation and it was accepted." In the last paragraph, the *Star Tribune* adopted the *Pioneer Press* half-truth version of the basis on which I had provided them with the documents:

> When Cohen last week gave at least three reporters copies of the court documents on Johnson, he asked that his name not be used. But both the *Minneapolis Star Tribune* and the *St. Paul Pioneer Press* identified Cohen as the person who provided the documents.

There was no mention of the promise made to me and broken. No mention of their reporter's refusal to lend her name to the article that named me. No mention of WCCO-TV and the AP having made the same promise the papers made to me and, unlike them, keeping their word. The author of the *Star Tribune* article was concealed.

On Tuesday, election day, the lead story in the Variety section of the *Star Tribune* was headlined, "If you think political mud got heavy, just look beyond Minnesota's borders." The article wound up,

> Every state has its stinkballs (or do I mean gunkheads) and there have been instances of whispering campaigns, name-calling and nasty, 11th hour leaking in Minnesota this year that I would def-

initely put in this category. ... I think it's wonderful that there's a place where mudslinging backfires.

In the *Pioneer Press*, where the coverage had been more restrained than in the *Star Tribune*, an editorial had appeared on October 29, titled "Relevant disclosures which appeared in the Pioneer Press." According to the editorial,

> Too much is being made by supporters of Rudy Perpich, the DFL candidate for governor, about Republican fingerprints on documents leaked to the press showing his running mate was convicted of shoplifting 12 years ago. ... To focus on how the information got to the public's attention is to overlook a larger issue. That is that the information about Lieutenant Governor candidate Marlene Johnson is something the voting public deserves to know. After all, if she is elected, she will be a Governor in waiting. ... Miss Johnson said she told Rudy Perpich about the incident earlier this year before he selected her as his running mate. The last-minute disclosure could have been avoided if Mr. Perpich and Ms. Johnson had informed the public themselves earlier and confronted the issue squarely.

In the election held on November 2, David Durenberger was reelected to the United States Senate over Mark Dayton 938,846 to 825,920.

The Perpich/Johnson ticket beat Whitney/Krenik 1,023,823 to 704,878.

My only prospect for any kind of a permanent job was lost.

There was other news of interest to me on election day. On the front page of the Metro section was a picture of Ron Edwards, next to a story headlined, "Ron Edwards' council support erodes."

Edwards's detractors on the council said that "Edwards' brand of confrontational politics, spawned in the '60s, is no longer effective in the '80s."

And there was John Cowles Jr., my nemesis from the Edwards case thirteen years earlier, still calling the shots at the paper. A headline on the front page of the *Star Tribune* that day read, "John Cowles Jr. fires publisher Dwight."

The story reported that "[Donald] Dwight's dismissal, which sources close to the publisher said came as a surprise to the 51-year-old executive, is the latest in a series of upheavals at Cowles Media and, its flagship Minneapolis newspaper, where earnings have been declining sharply for three years." Another anonymous source. I wondered why this one was able to stay that way.

CHAPTER NINE

Piling On

Needing work, I called Pat Fallon, who had once been my boss at Martin/Williams.

"Have you got anything over there?"

"No, but why don't you call Bob Rueff at Clark Livingston?" Prior to founding Fallon McElligott, Fallon and Rueff had been the nonsurvivors in a three-way struggle for the crown prince slot at Martin/Williams. The winner had been my former boss, Dave Floren.

A kind of underground railroad grew up. I was quietly passed from hand to hand by a few loyal friends. On Monday morning, I had temporary office space at Rueff's agency. His partner, Clark Livingston, had been willing to go along with it, but not for long. In return, I ran what little design and production work I had through the agency.

Fallon got me a freelance copywriting job doing a series of recruiting brochures for the University of Minnesota football program. Whitney hired me to work with Ismach to ghost some articles on health care. And Jim Dorr, a Democrat who had helped me earlier to become president of the city planning commission, walked into my office at Clark Livingston, check in hand, and asked me to prepare a marketing plan for his firm, Dayton's Commercial Interiors.

They were scraps, but I was grateful for whatever I could get. More important than the work itself was knowing there were still people who believed in me. It made it possible for me to believe in myself. I was going to survive somehow.

Meanwhile, though the election was over and the results would seem to have been what they had hoped for, the *Star Tribune* was ready to stamp out any lingering signs of life in the enemy camp.

On November 7, Flakne wrote a letter to the editor, the first time the paper's readers were informed that the paper had promised me anonymity. "Surely your paper did not need to breach its agreement with Cohen to confirm the truth of the information," wrote Flakne. "A minimal amount of investigation would have revealed the information was correct without revealing a confidential source."

Flakne's five-paragraph letter drew a twenty-five paragraph editorial response from Lou Gelfand, the readers' representative. Gelfand concluded that "publishing Cohen's name without his permission is justified by an unspoken standard of journalism that defines the substance of Cohen's tip as beneath the threshold of acceptable, unattributable information." Oh, I get it now. It didn't matter that the material I gave them was true, or that they had made a promise to me, or that they had broken the promise and then concealed it from their readers until a third party wrote in about it. It was all okay because accurate information concerning the arrest and conviction of a candidate for the state's second-highest office was "beneath the threshold."

I'd violated the "unspoken standard."

Two weeks later, someone tipped *Star Tribune* columnist Doug Grow that I had been working for the University. In his November 20 column titled, "'U' reticent about Cohen's role in writing recruiting flyers," Grow reverted to the original *Star Tribune* spin. There was no mention of the broken promise to me, even though Gelfand had admitted it two weeks earlier:

In giving the reporters the information, Cohen had requested that he remain anonymous. But editors at Minneapolis and St. Paul newspapers decided that the fact that Cohen was distributing the information in the last week of the election campaign was as important as the information he distributed.

Grow's article identified Paul Giel, the men's athletic director at the University, and Bob Geary, an assistant, as part of a cover-up. Fred Konrath, the recruiting coordinator, was forthcoming about my role. "I don't see any tie-in between what happened and what we are trying to do here," said Fred Konrath, recruiting coordinator for the Gopher football team. "We're just trying to improve upon some things and Dan does a good job."

Grow never identified the anonymous source for this story. Apparently, this information was not "beneath the threshold."

I'd had it.

The papers had lied to me and concealed their lie under a fog of bluster and self-righteousness. I had been fired from my job and now, weeks after the original story had ceased to be news, the *Star Tribune* was tracking down and harassing people whose only crime was to hire me so I could make a living again.

Enough was enough.

CHAPTER TEN

Enough is Enough

On Monday, November 22, two days after Grow's article appeared, I signed a retainer agreement with Charlie Hvass, a well-known Minneapolis plaintiff's tort attorney.

I had talked with two other lawyers before I hired Hvass. Flakne had indicated he wanted to represent me, but how could he? He would be a fact witness in the case. I also spoke with our family lawyer, who had extensive trial experience. While I never got to the point of asking him to take the case, he made it clear to me he didn't want to. He hinted that there wasn't enough in the way of potential recovery to interest him, but I've learned that the given reason is seldom the real reason. Like everyone else, he had followed the story in the *Star Tribune* and was quite aware of how the paper dealt with people who displeased them. I suspect that taking on the most powerful and possibly most hard-nosed and vindictive institution in town did not appeal to him as a wise career move.

With Hvass, it was strictly a business proposition. He had made his reputation representing the families of victims of airline disasters. These are relatively easy cases for a plaintiff's lawyer. There's no question of who's at fault, or the extent of the victim's injuries—they're dead, and there's never any contributory negligence.

Another characteristic that makes these accidents attractive to plaintiff's lawyers is that even more than most tort cases, they tend to get settled rather than tried. Plaintiff's lawyers can settle fifty cases in the time it takes to try one, and when they go to trial, they can always lose. Airlines do not care to have exhaustive testimony taken in a public courtroom regarding events that have taken scores of human lives and for which they are responsible. Hvass seldom had to go to trial in an airline accident case. He had a firm grasp of the economics of his practice. Hvass was a first-class money lawyer.

But as Hvass was soon to discover, suing a newspaper, particularly these newspapers under these circumstances, with me as his client, was a different proposition entirely.

The press occupies a unique position under our Constitution. The Founding Fathers were more fearful of tyranny than they were fond of order and harmony. They had fought and won the Revolutionary War to throw off the yoke of the British monarchy, and they were determined to avoid a repetition of that experience. They envisioned a free, disputatious, skeptical, robust, and uninhibited press as a watchdog of the people against the secret workings and excesses of government. The First Amendment codifies that view, providing "Congress shall make no law ... abridging ... the freedom of speech, or of the press."

A series of Supreme Court decisions has affirmed and expanded the press's rights. In *New York Times v. Sullivan,* the Court held that the First Amendment barred a public figure from recovery against the press in a libel action, even if the press had published libelous material about that person, absent a showing of actual malice, an almost impossible evidentiary hurdle. There had never been a case where a plaintiff had recovered damages because a news organization had broken its promise not to reveal the name of an individual as an anonymous source.

While the press has fulfilled its role as a check on the power of government, there has been little in the way of a check on the power of the press. In places like Minneapolis and St. Paul, competition has had only a limited effect. These are one-newspaper towns, and because television newscasts rarely cover any subject in depth, let alone editorialize, they tend to be one-opinion towns as well. The newspapers lay out the course, set the speed, and lead the way. The rest of the pack follows.

Another reason the newspapers get away with whatever they want is that these are also towns where conformity and respect for authority are bred into the bones of the citizenry. Given six months of winter and the largely homogeneous, largely northern European population, taciturnity is a cultural value here. High emotions are not. People here tend not to give each other the finger in traffic or tear up tickets, order something that isn't on the menu or send things back to the kitchen. It's similar to the venue Tom Wolfe described in his book *Radical Chic & Mau-Mauing the Flak Catchers.* The worst thing you can do is shout. Or argue. Or call attention to yourself.

Though the constitutional issues in my case were kicked back and forth in four different courts, resulting in five separate published opinions, the case was never really about the Constitution.

One court said, "Both parties tried to occupy the high moral ground."

Not at all.

Each party tried to make it impossible for the other party to occupy it.

I challenged the institutional integrity of the *Minneapolis Star Tribune* and the *St. Paul Pioneer Press.* I called them "liars" and "frauds." I accused them of "dishonesty" and "dirty tricks." And I did it in public, in a court of law, before a jury of their peers, and a national audience, and anyone who would listen to me. I shouted. I argued. I called attention to myself.

They did the same. They did it in their newspapers and their professional and trade association journals. They did it in concert with other newspapers, who closed ranks with them and filed friend-of-the-court briefs, supporting their position. They drew editorial cartoons of me in the guise of a human garbage can. They said I was "sleazy," a "dirty trickster," a "sham," a "stinkball," a "gunkhead." They ridiculed me, scoffed at my motives, gloated over my firing, harassed those with the temerity to hire me after my downfall.

This was not a lawsuit about money, or about constitutional principles.

It was about honor.

Neither of us could lose and be the same as we were before.

Hvass had given my case the once-over and noted the obvious. The *Star Tribune* and the *Pioneer Press* were big outfits with lots of money. They just might be willing to settle for the nuisance value if I would go away. Soon enough, it became clear to Hvass that he was dealing with a determined opponent, and that it was I, and not the newspapers, who was going to be the bigger nuisance so far as he was concerned.

Though I was not aware that Charlie Hvass's agenda might be different from my own, I was uneasy with him from the outset. On December 22, a month after I had hired him, I wrote a letter to our family lawyer:

> When I was in your office Monday to sign the Pacific Stock Exchange papers, I wanted to tell you a curious feature of my arrangement with Charlie, but because you were on the phone, I never got the chance.
>
> Charlie agreed to take the case on a one-third contingency fee basis during a phone conversation I had with him on Friday, November 19. He asked me to come to the office the next Monday morning to discuss the case. There were three people present: Charlie, his administrative assistant Liz Haugen, and me. Charlie started to tell me his theory of the case. I interrupted after awhile to ask if some sort of conspiracy allegation was appropriate. He explained it was not. I recited a long list of miscellaneous points. Liz Haugen took notes. Charlie wound up with a somewhat emotional recitation of what he would

attempt to accomplish—to force them to admit they were wrong.

For the first time since the event, I felt a kind of emotional catharsis, as if a burden were being lifted from my shoulders. When he said the word "wrong," I began to sob, not loudly, but unmistakably, shielding my eyes with my hand. It lasted about a minute. Charlie handed me a Kleenex, said, rather coolly I thought, "You've been under a great emotional strain," and handed me the enclosed document. He explained it, saying that if there were no recovery, there would be no cost to me. I asked him about the paragraph dealing with expenses. He said they "had never tried to collect them in cases they lost," but they were "required" to have that language in the agreement.

I was too addled to ask who or what required it, and I lacked the presence of mind to ask, "What happens if you die and your successor claims no knowledge of this arrangement?" or for that matter, if I die and there is no record of this conversation?

It bothers me, but I am reluctant to raise the point with Charlie. Frankly, he intimidates me a little and I don't want to upset the applecart. In fact, I'm reluctant to tell you, machoism I suppose.

So here's my record of that conversation and my copy of the agreement. I'm not asking you to do anything more but hang on to it for whatever purpose it might serve in the future.

Dan Cohen

CHAPTER ELEVEN

Goodbye, Charlie

On December 16, 1982, I sued the Cowles Media Company, the parent of the *Minneapolis Star Tribune*, and Northwest Publications, parent of the *St. Paul Pioneer Press*, for breach of contract and misrepresentation. I asked for compensatory damages in excess of $50,000, and punitive damages in excess of $50,000. In her answer, the *Star Tribune's* in-house lawyer, Patricia Hirl, denied all our substantive allegations but one.

> [The *Star Tribune*] admits that on Wednesday, October 27, 1982, Lori Sturdevant, an agent of *Star* and *Tribune*, indicated to Plaintiff that Plaintiff would not be identified as the source of said information and that his identity would be kept anonymous.

In the *Pioneer Press's* answer to the complaint, David Seykora, an attorney at the white-shoe Oppenheimer law firm, made the same admission in slightly different language.

> Plaintiff offered to furnish and did furnish information to one of its employees on October 27, 1982, that the Plaintiff requested that his name not be used, and that the employee promised not to use his name.

Like the *Star Tribune*, the *Pioneer Press* denied the other substantive allegations. Unlike the *Star Tribune*, they threw in a gratuitous insult: a demand for payment of attorney's fees by me "for assertion of claims in bad faith."

I was obsessed with the case and began to besiege Hvass with notes, memos, letters, unannounced visits. His administrative assistant, Liz Haugen, caught my incessant calls and handled them with courtesy and patience. Underlying all this activity was the message: let's get the show on the road.

Hvass grew increasingly unhappy with me.

On July 15, 1983, seven months after the case was filed, he gently tried to stem the torrent:

> I note that you are apprehensive from time to time about what is going on in your case. As I tell all of my clients, if I continually brought every client up-to-date on what I am doing, I would never have time to do anything.
>
> Each item that is mailed in to me is read, either by me or by Liz and Liz will then point out to me the pertinent or relative portion of the newspaper article, etc., that may apply in your case.

It didn't work. I turned up the volume another notch. Hvass's patience began to wear thin.

On September 18, 1984, nearly two years after we had started the suit, he wrote me:

> I'm not coming at you from a moral standpoint, I do wish you would tone down your letters. The language used in the letters is reviewed by Betty, my secretary, by Liz, and by me. It's language that I do not tolerate around the law firm and for someone with such a great command of the English language, it doesn't do anything for you. You can think the words, just don't put them in print.

That didn't work either, though I never again used the offending word, *shit*, in a letter to Hvass. Then came the turning point in our relationship. We got into a protracted disagreement about expenses. Two days after the "no shit" letter, I received another letter from Hvass's office, this time from Robert King Jr., who had been taking depositions in the case. He enclosed a bill for costs incurred and told me Hvass wanted me to "bring this account current."

I sent both Hvass and King a copy of the letter I'd sent two years earlier to our family lawyer, in which I'd quoted Hvass as having said when we entered into our fee arrangement that "if there were no recovery there would be no cost to me," and the firm "never tried to collect them [fees] in cases they lost."

It was clear from my letter I had anticipated problems with Hvass from the moment I had hired him, and had made my doubts known to another lawyer almost immediately. It was not a flattering appraisal.

Hvass tried to temporize. On September 24, he wrote me:

> We currently have about $1,300.00 on the books and I am willing to let that abide the outcome of the lawsuit. However, the firm has instructed me that no more costs are to be incurred in connection with your matter unless they are prepaid by you.

> I suggest that we have a prepayment for expenses with you and an agreement that as we contemplate incurring further expenses, we *contact you in advance* for your approval, otherwise we do not incur them.

That letter only led to further disagreements. King subsequently tried to collect an additional $1,000 in expenses from me about which I had not been contacted in advance. I refused to pay them.

Hvass had had enough. He tried to settle the case. In April 1985, Hvass, Hirl, and Seykora began an extensive correspondence.

Hvass asked me to come to his office on December 31, 1985. I had seen enough of Hvass in action to spot a "tell," a poker expression for a mannerism that indicated an opponent was telegraphing the contents of his hand. When Hvass really got into it, he would assume an elaborate air of casualness, tilting far back in his chair, putting his hands behind his head and turning sideways, not directly addressing the person across his desk.

Hvass tilted back his chair a little, faced sideways, and said, "I've been discussing a settlement with the papers."

The proposed settlement involved payment to me of $2,000 from each paper and a statement from the parties to be published in the papers announcing the disposition of the case. The statement was unremarkable except for one feature. Despite the pittance I was to receive, Seykora proposed a version that ended with: "Cohen received no money from either paper."

I couldn't believe what I was hearing.

For three years, I'd been trying to lift the cloud of humiliation that hovered over me. I was desperate for my day in court, where I could be vindicated. For three years, I'd been trying to light a fire under Hvass. Instead, Hvass was urging me to settle the case for $4,000.

Not even that.

There's the one-third of that amount he would receive as his fee under our retainer agreement and the $1,300 in expenses on his books, plus another $1,000 in expenses that were in dispute, leaving me with somewhere between $100 and $1,400, less than what I would have been paid for three years' work if I'd been stamping out license plates at the state pen.

I didn't care to go through life as the man with the $100 reputation.

I turned it down out of hand.

Hvass's chair went into full tilt, he put his hands behind his head, and he played his ace:

"Robert King and I have spoken about the case, and Robert feels that if you refuse to accept the settlement, we should resign the case."

The retainer agreement provided that the firm "reserves the right to withdraw as my counsel and terminate any attorney-client relationship at any time."

"Your resignation is accepted," I said.

Now what the hell would I do?

CHAPTER TWELVE

Hello, Elliot

There wasn't exactly a long line of applicants to take over the case from Hvass.

Minneapolis is your classic flyover city, a frozen tundra four hundred miles from anyplace else of comparable size, and out of the mainstream of East-West traffic. The newspapers ran the show, and they made sure everyone knew it. To take on the papers was to risk pissing off the largest, most influential, and vocal institutions in town. Judges-in-waiting, which is to say, most lawyers, do not take such matters lightly.

Hvass had thought it was worth a try, but when he realized that there would be no quick settlement, he cut his losses.

I was going to have to find someone with a less pragmatic approach, someone who harbored a deep-seated hatred of the newspapers, someone with nothing to lose.

Someone like me.

During the time my relationship with Hvass was nearing its grand finale, I met several times with another lawyer who was writing an article about the case.

Elliot Rothenberg was a Jewish Republican, Harvard Law grad who did some writing. He was three years younger than me and lived a mile from where I lived. He'd been an elected public official, serving in the state legislature from the district next to mine.

Rothenberg had run for attorney general of Minnesota in 1982, the same time Whitney was running for governor. He'd lost to Hubert Humphrey III. The paper not only had endorsed Humphrey, but went beyond its usual distaste for all things Republican in ridiculing Rothenberg's candidacy.

It seemed like a pretty good match. I asked him to represent me.

"There could be a problem," he said.

"What's that?"

"I used to be married to Patricia Hirl."

"If it's not a problem for you, it's not a problem for me," I said.

It was, however, a problem for the *Star Tribune*. After Rothenberg wrote an article for the *Columbia Journalism Review*, in which he supported me and criticized the papers who'd blown my cover, Joel Kramer, the *Star Tribune's* new executive editor, wrote a letter to the editor of the *Columbia Journalism Review*:

> A dart to CJR editors for allowing Elliot C. Rothenberg to write "No Way to Treat a Tipster" (January/February 1986), an article that portrays political consultant Dan Cohen in a favorable light and the two Twin Cities dailies unfavorably.

> Far from a disinterested observer, Rothenberg was an unsuccessful candidate for state office on the same ticket which Cohen was trying to aid. He is also the divorced husband of the *Star and Tribune* counsel who has been handling this case from the beginning. The article made no mention of these connections.

The *Star Tribune* obviously had decided it would take no unanswered blows. My defenders would also be subject to at least a whiff of the garbage can treatment. Rothenberg had remarried by this time, and Hirl was engaged. Whatever exchanges they had on the case were completely lawyerlike.

There was still fallout from my dealings with Hvass. King had told me he had filed a certificate of readiness with the court in March 1985. Filing this document is tantamount to asking for a date for trial. When Rothenberg got my files from Hvass's office, he discovered the original copy of the certificate of readiness. I was furious. On March 13, 1986, I wrote Hvass and King:

> Once Elliot told you [the certificate] wasn't [filed], you had neither the courage nor the courtesy to apologize—or even tell me directly. ...
>
> What did you intend to do, wait until the defendants filed a motion to dismiss for failure to prosecute and then try to panic me into a settlement?
>
> I don't think you filed the certificate because I don't think you ever intended to try this case.
>
> I await your prompt answer as I consider taking action in this matter.

I never got one. I brought a complaint against Hvass before the state lawyers' disciplinary board. They ruled against me and for Hvass, saying:

> The new attorney discovered that the certificate of readiness had not been filed and contacted Mr. King. When Mr. King examined the file he found this to be true. He admitted in a letter to the new attorney that his office had made an error. Court procedures are such that this oversite [sic] should not seriously affect the outcome of the case and should not cause the new attorney problems.

In sending me the results of their investigation, the state board erroneously included their findings in another complaint. I wrote them back: "Unfortunately—for me—your carelessness in mailing this material to me seems to be a metaphor for your overall handling of this matter." I appealed their ruling and lost that, too.

I wasn't through yet. I still had to deal with King's continued attempts to collect $2,300 in expenses. I asked for a hearing before the county bar association committee on fees.

As Hvass, King, and I waited outside the hearing room, Hvass reached out his hand and said, "Dan, I want you to know my hand is always out to you in friendship."

"Charlie, your hand is always out, but not in friendship."

The county committee ruled while we were still in the hearing room. They knocked out the $1,000 that had been run up by King without consulting me in advance, and they enforced Hvass's earlier assurance to me that the remaining $1,300 would abide the outcome of the lawsuit.

I never saw Hvass again.

Hooking up with Rothenberg hadn't improved my behavior. I called him on a daily basis. He worked out of his home, by himself, without a secretary, so he learned early in the game never to pick up his phone until he could be sure I wasn't the caller. As a result, I fulminated endlessly into his answering machine. It worked for him and it worked for me. I had my catharsis. He didn't have to respond—or even listen—just erase the tape and start over the next day.

Rothenberg's approach was different from that of Hvass and King in other ways, too. Before the defendants began my deposition, Hvass had given me the traditional lawyer's counsel: say as little as possible. I ignored his advice, blathering endlessly and driving King nuts. He recessed the deposition to chew me out. I kept talking. Eventually, even the lawyers for the other side tried to shut me up. Unsuccessfully. When Rothenberg took over, however, he used the laissez-faire approach. Why get upset? I kept blabbing no matter what anyone said to me.

As we approached trial, Hirl left the case. The new counsel for the *Star Tribune* was James Fitzmaurice, chief litigator for Faegre & Benson, a powerhouse firm that represented Cowles Media, Norwest Bank, Dayton Hudson, and many of the state's largest corporations.

Paul Hannah, an experienced trial attorney with the local Oppenheimer firm, replaced David Seykora. Shortly afterward,

Hannah left Oppenheimer to start his own practice. He continued to represent the St. Paul papers. On July 5, 1988, the trial of *Cohen v. Cowles Media and Northwest Publications* began in Hennepin County District Court, Judge Franklin P. Knoll presiding.

CHAPTER THIRTEEN

Dirty Tricks

It had taken nearly six years for me to get my day in court. Now that I was there, it looked like we were overmatched.

Despite our fancy educations and modest accomplishments, the glory days had long since passed for both Rothenberg and me. We were deep into middle age and making marginal livings on the fringes of our professions. Rothenberg was a sole practitioner. For a long time, I was his only client.

One of the countless things we needed for the trial was an expert witness, someone who could testify from our perspective about newspaper practices dealing with anonymous sources, since the defendants were sure to produce their own experts to claim they had acted properly. I got turned down over and over again. Austin Wehrwein, a retired *Star* editorial writer who had once won a Pulitzer Prize, was more candid than most who declined the honor.

"You won't get anybody," he said, "we're all afraid of them."

He was almost right. I was turned down by Steve Alness, former editorial editor of the *Star;* Don Gilmor, the faculty specialist on communication law at the University of Minnesota School of Journalism; and Father James Whalen, head of the journalism department at the University of St. Thomas.

I talked with Mitch Charnley, a retired journalism professor at the University of Minnesota. When I was an undergraduate, I had written an article about Tom Heggen, the author of a collection of short stories entitled *Mr. Roberts* and an old student of

Charnley's. He had called me to tell me he liked it, and he had it reprinted in a supplement to the University's paper, the *Minnesota Daily*. By the time of the trial, Charnley was in his eighties. I'm not sure if he would have done it or not. I didn't quite ask him.

Instead, we got Bernard Casserly as our expert witness. Casserly was no spring chicken, either. He was in his late sixties, and editor emeritus of the *Catholic Bulletin*, from which he had retired as editor six years earlier. He had worked for the *Star* and *Tribune* as a reporter many years before that. He was still writing columns for Catholic publications.

In the meantime, I became my own research assistant and investigator. I spent countless hours at the Minneapolis and St. Paul public libraries combing old newspapers and moldy clipping files for anything we could use. On the rare occasions when I actually saw Rothenberg, I would go to his home and ring the doorbell, and he would shuffle up from his basement office in a torn T-shirt or tatty bathrobe, fumble with the lock, and try to get his goofy springer spaniel under control. I would pass him whatever documents I had brought through a crack in the doorway, and he would disappear back into his lair. Rothenberg was brilliant, but he was strange. He disliked the defendants as passionately as I did, blaming them for his defeat at the hands of Hubert Humphrey III and for the double standard by which he felt Republicans, especially Jewish Republicans, were judged. He was tireless, fearless, and focused, and he was delighted at the opportunity to finally confront his tormentors on what we hoped would be a level playing field.

We were like two guys from Pinsk who had been petitioning the government for years and had finally been ordered to come to the capital to air our grievances.

We didn't know whether they were going to give us medals or hang us.

Whichever it was, we would be dressed for the occasion. I bought three suits, bringing my total to four. After forty years of crew cuts, I decided to wear my hair—what there was of it—slicked back, lounge-lizard style. I thought it looked more businesslike. For his part, Rothenberg got new suits, too. His wife had given him a shiny new briefcase with his initials stamped on it in gold. This was a marked improvement over the FedEx envelopes he normally used for carrying papers, but it didn't convey the impression of an experienced, ring-wise litigator.

The first thing to do at a trial is to pick a jury. This is done through a process called voir dire. A panel of prospective jurors is seated in the jury box. The judge asks them questions. Then counsel for each side asks them questions. If a prospective juror indicates he or she has formed an opinion about the case or knows or has a relationship to one of the parties, that person can be eliminated for cause. Judges generally will act on their own accord in these cases, sparing counsel the possibility of retaliation from another prospective juror who may have formed a friendship with the person dismissed.

Each side also has three peremptory challenges. Lawyers save them for cases where they can't challenge for cause, but have a strong hunch the juror is not going to vote right. These are written on a slip of paper, identified by location—"third juror from the left in the front row"—and handed to the judge, so no prospective jurors know which side bumped them. Rothenberg and I had a pretty good idea of what we were looking for in a juror. More specifically, what we were *not* looking for: Jews and/or liberal Republicans.

Given a Jewish plaintiff with a Jewish lawyer, a Jewish jury member will tend to bend over backward to show he or she isn't representative of the they-all-stick-together stereotype.

As for liberal Republicans, I was mindful of Gene McCarthy's aphorism: "A liberal Republican is someone who, if he sees you drowning twenty feet offshore, will toss you a rope

ten feet long and say he's met you halfway." Another case where
a juror might be likely to dump on me in order to prove his or
her impartiality.

The judge was a great help here. He had been a pol. Like
many of his brethren on the bench, Frank Knoll was a judge
because he was a lawyer who knew a governor. He had been a
Democratic state senator before he was appointed by Rudy
Perpich.

He told an anti-Reagan joke. Only two prospective jurors,
both from wealthy Minneapolis suburbs, laughed. They made our
pre-empt list. No Rockefeller Republicans need apply.

The defendants also had definite ideas about what they wanted. They wanted women.

It took about two hours to select the jury. Our six-person
jury—allowed by Minnesota law—was made up of four women
and two men. They were all working people. Four of them were
in their forties or older. Minnesota law also permits a five-sixths
jury verdict. Either side could win, even if there was a holdout.
The judge gave the jury general instructions: "be impartial,"
"keep an open mind," "be attentive," expect "vigorous cross-
examination." Then he called on Rothenberg to give his opening statement, which would give the jurors a preview of the evidence that the lawyer planned to present during the trial.

Rothenberg went through the whole megillah from the day
I spent with John Y. Brown to the meeting with Flakne and company, the meetings with the reporters, the broken promise, the
inconsistency of the paper in letting Sturdevant withdraw her
name and remain anonymous as "Staff Writer" while I was left
slowly twisting in the wind.

He described the *Star Tribune's* campaign of vilification and
how it continued after the election. As recently as a few weeks
before the trial—and six years after the actual event—Paul
Hannah, the *Pioneer Press* lawyer, had gone after me personally in
an article in the *Washington Post*. Rothenberg cited examples

where the papers had honored promises of anonymity, where they had editorialized against shoplifting, where they had revealed shoplifting convictions about public figures and criticized their conduct, where they published last-minute revelations about candidates.

When Rothenberg finally finished, it was late in the afternoon. The court recessed. Fitzmaurice and Hannah made their opening statements the next morning.

Fitzmaurice didn't fool around. He went for the gut. "We're not going to supply you with a bunch of information that will confuse you," he said. He was as good as his word. During the course of his brief presentation he expressly referred to my behavior as a dirty trick six times:

My early morning meeting with Flakne and the other Republicans was to plot a "dirty trick."

Getting Lori Sturdevant to make a promise was a "dirty trick." Lori Sturdevant was "from South Dakota" and had "worked on several small-town newspapers." I was the sophisticate who had attended Stanford and Harvard Law School.

"Did Dan Cohen come forth and say, 'Lori, I have some information, I want to share the information with you, let me give you an idea of what it is?' He didn't do that. He got the promise, he got the commitment, he got her to say okay."

If I hadn't made them give me a promise, they wouldn't have had to break it. That explains why, in their answer to our complaint, the defendants admitted they had promised me anonymity.

As soon as the editors saw it, they realized it was a "real dirty trick."

So they sent a reporter over to the courthouse to see who had checked out the record on Marlene Johnson, and when they saw it was Flakne, it "started to smell like dirty tricks."

And when I told Floren about it that afternoon, he was too stunned to speak, because this was a "real dirty trick."

Fitzmaurice summed up the dirty trick theme by saying:

> Why was it a dirty trick? Well, what about the rights of Marlene Johnson? Here was a woman from a humble background, who had pulled herself up by her own bootstraps, and six days before the election, about to become the next lieutenant governor, if the polls are correct, and suddenly someone wants to dump this out as news.

And once I was told that the editors had overruled Sturdevant and decided to print the story with my name in it, what did I do? Instead of having "given it up for what it was, a dirty trick," I attacked both Johnson and Perpich for "living a lie."

Where Rothenberg had been earnest and workmanlike, Fitzmaurice had been dramatic. He had a thing he did with his glasses. They were half-glasses with a black leather strap that dangled from the bottom of the earpieces and contrasted with the lighter-colored suits he wore. He would peer over the tops, or lift off the glasses and let them drop across his chest, or prop them up on his forehead. Even when he wasn't flourishing them as a stage prop—he probably had better vision than Ted Williams did the year he hit .406—I was always conscious of the position of the glasses and would check them out during dull moments. Fitzmaurice knew how to get your attention.

He moved around the courtroom with ease and assurance. Rothenberg was awkward and hesitant. But so what? Fitzmaurice was smarmy. Rothenberg was sincere. But would the jury see it that way?

Hannah was next. His presentation was cut from the same cloth as Fitzmaurice's, softened somewhat by an occasional reference to the facts. He told the jury to look for hooks, which he defined as "interesting concepts." The first hook would be "the promise." The second hook would be "the decision." "At the end when the lawyers all summarize what happened," said Hannah, he would discuss the significance of what had been learned about the hooks.

Rothenberg's turn again. He called his first witness.

Me.

CHAPTER FOURTEEN

Opprobrium

There had been a lot of pretrial publicity and the courtroom was crowded. There were the usual family members—my wife attended every session and my daughters, Ruth Ann and Polly, attended most of them—as well as a larger-than-usual number of courtroom buffs and reporters. Despite the air conditioning, it was hot, and from time to time the judge would interrupt the trial and order the doors thrown open to let some fresh air in or ask people standing in the back of the room to take seats or he would arrange for more chairs. Just before I began to testify, the judge gave Fitzmaurice permission to introduce his client to the jury. It turned out to be Tim McGuire, managing editor at the *Star Tribune*.

McGuire was no more Fitzmaurice's client than Lori Sturdevant or Joel Kramer, the editor, or Roger Parkinson, the publisher, or John Cowles Jr., the man whose name was on the complaint. The idea was to give the big, impersonal corporation a sympathetic human face. McGuire was small and vulnerable looking. His hands were slightly deformed from a birth defect. For the first week of the trial, he sat at the defendant's table, taking notes.

I was sworn in and took the witness stand.

Rothenberg went through the basics, handling the stigma of my having attended Harvard Law School by asking me if I recognized anyone else in the room who had gone there.

"Yes, you and Paul Hannah."

He asked me whether I had known of the existence of the court document before my meeting with Flakne and company.

"No," I testified. His questioning continued:

> Q: (by Rothenberg): Had you known of any conviction of Ms. Johnson for theft before you saw these documents?
>
> A: (by Cohen): No, sir. No, sir.
>
> Q: Any particular reason why you didn't give it either to the *Star & Tribune* or the *Pioneer Press* as a scoop, or let them get a scoop, as opposed to giving it to four?
>
> A: Sure. I felt no obligation to give it to one of these media exclusively for the benefit of one at the expense of the other, or just for the benefit of one. I didn't have any reason to give one an advantage over any other one.

Rothenberg went over my meeting with Sturdevant. I emphasized that she had not asked for exclusivity and that as I was leaving, she had said "something to the effect that 'this is the sort of thing that I'd like to have you bring by again if you ever have anything like it.'"

After Rothenberg finished with my meeting with Sturdevant, he went over my conversation with Salisbury:

> Q: And did [Salisbury] express his appreciation for you giving the materials to him?
>
> A: He said, "This is political dynamite."

Rothenberg concluded my direct testimony by giving me a chance to do a long riff on dirty tricks, and why the papers had played one on me, rather than my having played one on them. I said what they had done was "wrong," "immoral," and I was "outraged" by it.

In the end, Rothenberg had gotten into evidence most of what we had hoped to get in. But there was a problem. He wasn't comfortable in the courtroom. There was a fixed procedure for offering evidence, and more than once he stumbled over the rules while the judge rolled his eyes and painstakingly reminded him of the correct procedure.

My wife and older daughter began to pass me notes during the recesses: "Tell Elliot to get the evidence marked before he tries to introduce it." I nodded solemnly and stuck the notes in my pocket. He was doing just fine for a guy who may or may not have been trying a case before a jury for the first time in his life— he never quite answered me when I asked him about his trial experience—particularly for someone going up against a couple of pros, one of whom, Fitzmaurice, was listed in the book *The Best Lawyers in America.*

I wasn't so sure about my own performance.

It was the defendant's turn to question me. Fitzmaurice produced a document, had it marked, and thrust it into my hand. His cross-examination followed:

> Q: (by Fitzmaurice): I hand you, sir, a document which I will represent to you [as] the Code of Professional Responsibility for the practice which you engage in, that is, public relations; you agree with that?
> A: No.

There was a long exchange about the document, which was finally received in evidence over Rothenberg's objections. It ran about thirteen typed, single-spaced pages. I had never seen it before. It was published by the Public Relations Society of America. I wasn't a member. Fitzmaurice finally backed off a bit from questioning me about it and agreed to "make a copy available to you overnight; you can take all the time you want to read it and review it, study it, and then we'll have a visit about it in the morning."

> A: Okay.
> Q: And do you consider it part of your code of conduct in practicing your craft to deceive?
> A: No, sir.

Fitzmaurice continued in the same vein, going through the Fawkes Building meeting at length, painting the classic picture of the smoke-filled room. A gang of seedy old pols plotting to besmirch the reputation of the fair-haired damsel. You could practically hear the whistle of the train as we tied her to the railroad tracks.

> Q: Well, what were the cons? Who advocated any con?
> A: Well—
> Q: I suggest—
> A: Let me attempt—I can only answer one question at a time. Let me attempt to answer that. I recall expressing some skepticism about this, saying that I had just been involved in a campaign myself, and that information of a similar nature, more serious nature, actually, involving an opponent of mine in that election had come to my attention, and that I didn't really expect anybody to be terribly interested in this information, and I regarded that as being something of a negative, that it wasn't terribly interesting. In fact, the greatest enthusiasm I ever heard expressed for it was that expressed by Mr. Salisbury.
> Q: Do you know what a dirty trick is in the political sense?
> A: Yes, sir. I think it is when someone doesn't tell you the truth after they've made an agreement with you.
> Q: I meant more in the political sense.
> A: I do too, sir.

Shortly after this exchange, Fitzmaurice went into my job history. When he got to my tour of duty as an in-house writer at Lerner Publications, Rothenberg objected, trying to block disclosure of my having been fired. Our claim for damages included mental anguish. I had been upset and seen a psychiatrist a couple of times after I was fired, and we had given his report to defendants during the discovery phase of the case. There was an exchange at the bench, out of hearing of the jury.

MR. FITZMAURICE: Now he wants to open the door to mental anguish and the rest of it. We have a psychiatric report in here that indicates that Mr. Cohen, as a matter of personality, puts himself into dilemmas where he is almost achieving success, and then when he almost gets there, he just blows it up.

Fitzmaurice was too close to the truth for comfort. We dropped any claims of mental anguish.

Fitzmaurice asked me why I left Lerner. I said I was fired. That was that. No mental anguish. No psychiatrist's report.

The day wound up with some inconclusive sparring over the meaning of *exclusivity,* and the judge recessed the trial until the next morning.

I was beat. Beat and beat up. And I still had five hours of work to attend to that evening, for an advertising client. And when I was done, there was still the "Code of Professional Responsibility."

Fitzmaurice had told me to "take all the time you want to read it and review it, study it, and then we'll have a visit about it in the morning." I wasn't looking forward to it.

I should have known that Fitzmaurice wouldn't do what I expected him to do. The next morning, instead of starting with the "Code of Professional Responsibility," he went over the Sturdevant meeting again. Fitzmaurice asked me whether I thought that Sturdevant had "at any time made fraudulent representations."

MR. ROTHENBERG: Objection, Your Honor. That's calling for a legal conclusion, one of the issues in this case.
THE COURT: Sorry, but I'll have to have the question read. Would you read the question again?
(Whereupon, the record was read back.)
THE COURT: Mr. Cohen is a graduate of Harvard Law School, as I understand it?

I laughed.

> MR. ROTHENBERG: Your Honor, he's here as a Plaintiff, not an attorney in this case.
>
> THE COURT: Just a second. Do you find something amusing, Mr. Cohen?
>
> THE WITNESS: I apologize, sir. It's been 27 years since I graduated from the Harvard Law School. I've heard it more often in this courtroom the last few days than I had ever heard it before, so I guess—
>
> THE COURT: You certainly weren't laughing at my ruling, I take it?
>
> THE WITNESS: I apologize.
>
> THE COURT: That objection is overruled.

God, what had I done? Now I'd pissed off the judge. I was afraid to look at the jury.

Fitzmaurice repeated the question.

I answered, saying, in effect, I didn't have a clue whether she had made a fraudulent misrepresentation because "I can't reach a legal conclusion to that because it is a matter beyond my ability to analyze."

Next stop: my dealings with my old boss at Martin/Williams, Dave Floren. Fitzmaurice produced a memo Floren had written on October 28, the day after I had told him about my having provided the Johnson documents to the press.

> Q: It reads, in part, does it not,
>
> Yesterday afternoon when you told me of your role in the Johnson matter, there was no time to discuss how your action might affect Martin/Williams. In fact, you were obviously seeking no counsel on the matter, the deal had already been done. Since then, it has occurred to me there are two potentially serious ways in which what you have done can affect M/W as an ongoing successful business. The first, and of greatest consequence, is the effect your action will have on our own employees. … But the major concern, or the first concern that was expressed to you by Mr. Floren in the memo and later in dis-

cussions, was that your credibility among your co-workers was in serious jeopardy for having done this.

A: No, sir. The first concern Mr. Floren expressed in this memo was that he didn't have time to discuss my action the previous day. He's making it perfectly clear that after I had spoken with him about this that he made no response, and rather than covering myself as you suggested in some of your previous questions, this is a memorandum that looks like Mr. Floren is covering himself by saying that he felt there was no time to discuss my action.

Q: Are you suggesting, sir, that Mr. Floren would have sanctioned this conduct by you had he know about it in advance?

A: Sir, I told Mr. Floren about this when I got back to the office and Mr. Floren said nothing about it. That was my testimony, and ... that's what he's saying, here in this memo ... This memo ... is devised to cover himself.

Q: What the memo says next is ...

There was more memo, and more memo give-and-take along the same lines, but for once, I knew I had scored. Anyone who works in an office, and all our jurors did, knows enough about office politics to read Floren's memo for what it was: an ass-saver. Finally, Fitzmaurice trotted out the long-awaited "Code" for an encore.

Q: Would you turn to page 12, which is under the heading "An Official Interpretation of the Code as It Applies to Political Public Relations."

A: Yes, I see that.

Q: Then under that there are various precepts stated, and one of the precepts stated is item four, which reads:

Members shall not issue descriptive material or any advertising or publicity information, or participate in the preparation or use thereof, that is not signed by a responsible person, or is false, misleading or unlabeled as to its source, and are obligated to use care to avoid dissemination of any such material.

Now, sir, do you agree with that precept?

A: Within the context of other precepts, such as ... members shall respect the confidentiality of information pertaining to employers or clients, past, present and potential.

Within the context of a lot of the other precepts here, such as, "the statement of the truth," ... I think many of these principles are fine things.

It was nearly midnight when I had finally read the damn code and underlined "confidentiality of information" and "statement of the truth," which I took totally out of context and practically screamed from the witness stand. That was the last I heard of the "Code."

Fitzmaurice went back to my deposition. At that time, I had been asked, "And what was it about the revelation of your identity that caused you concern?"

A: I think that were my identity revealed because I was the messenger of ill tidings, that the public, my employer, the press, the world at large, would heap opprobrium on my head.

Q: That was your testimony?

A: Yes, sir.

Q: And the word that you selected to use as to what would befall you was opprobrium, right?

A: Yes, sir.

Q: O-p-p-r-o-b-r-I-u-m. That was the word that you selected, correct?

A: That's correct, sir.

Q: Now, I would like to hand you a copy of the Webster's New Collegiate Dictionary and ask you if you would look up the word opprobrium as it's defined in the dictionary.

A: Got it.

Q: Would you be kind enough to read it?

A: Opprobrium, for the Latin opprobrare: to reproach, for the French, or something. ... In the way of. Opprobrium. Reproach. Akin to Latin pro forward and to the Latin to carry, bring. ... 1: something that brings disgrace; 2 a: public disgrace or ill fame that follows from conduct considered grossly wrong or vicious, infamy; b. contempt, reproach, disgrace.

As I was reading, Fitzmaurice went over to a blackboard facing the jury box and picked up a piece of chalk. With a great flourish, he wrote *OPPROBRIUM* on it in big, bold letters.

That concluded my visit with James Fitzmaurice.

Except for the final zinger, I felt I gave as well as I got.

But so what? Even if I had held my own, what did I gain? A tactical standoff at best. The only thing that mattered was the strategic result: what impression had I made on the jury?

Fitzmaurice was a very, very smart lawyer. I had responded to many of his questions with hairsplitting, smarty-pants answers. Maybe he had even let me win a few to make me appear argumentative and arrogant and lose the sympathy of the jury.

We had sounded exactly like what we were: two lawyers quibbling over words and scoring debating points off each other. If I were to win this case, the jury would have to feel I had been wronged. They would have to like me.

I didn't feel I had achieved that. If I won, it would be despite my testimony, not because of it.

CHAPTER FIFTEEN

The Dog That Didn't Bark

After Fitzmaurice was through questioning me, it was Paul Hannah's turn. Fitzmaurice hadn't left much for him to do. We got into a silly exchange about whether or not Gary Flakne had chaired the meeting at Whitney headquarters. He went over my meeting with Salisbury and established that my state of mind was that Salisbury had told me the truth.

Then he asked me about exclusivity.

> Q: (by Hannah): Did you tell [Salisbury] that you had already given the information to Lori Sturdevant?
>
> A: I did not, nor was I asked.
>
> Q: Did you tell him that you planned to give the information to reporters from the Associated Press and WCCO?
>
> A: It didn't seem important enough to Mr. Salisbury to ask me. I did not tell him that, nor did Mr. Salisbury tell me, I might add, that apparently there's some hitch between him and his editors that allegedly requires him to consult with them on these matters. I told him exactly what I told you I told him.

Why did Hannah decide to go over exclusivity again? He was a good enough lawyer to know what my answers would be. The issue had been covered in the depositions, in my direct testimony, and in Fitzmaurice's cross-examination.

But there it was, and I was delighted. I couldn't see how it would help defendants with the jury. To most people a promise is a promise, a deal is a deal. When you buy a car, the dealer isn't about to throw in a free set of radials because you forgot to ask for them before you signed the papers.

But that isn't how the defendants saw it. They kept going back to exclusivity over and over, as if it were enough that because they had *assumed* exclusivity, they were entitled to act as if they had it. Their reporters had been sloppy, and they hadn't asked for it. It wasn't my fault that it wasn't part of the deal.

All right, then. It *should have* been part of the deal. And because it should have, and wasn't, the papers didn't have to keep their word. So they reneged. The crafty political operative had manipulated them, played a dirty trick, by shrewdly enticing their naïve and trusting reporters into a one-sided deal.

After all, didn't I realize these were newspapers? And because of the First Amendment, newspapers don't have to play by the same rules as the rest of us. That's the mind-set on press row. And they can't quite see why the rest of the world doesn't get with the program and see it the same way.

Exclusivity, or rather, the lack of it—not poor, innocent Marlene Johnson or the public's right to know—was the real reason we were sitting in that courtroom, each trying to convince the jury that the other side were moral lepers.

If I hadn't taken the slip of paper with the four reporters' names on it and trotted around the Twin Cities passing out envelopes like a FedEx deliveryman, probably none of it would have happened. However, there was another alternative to passing out the information in person, and Hannah was headed in that direction.

> Q: Now, Mr. Cohen, had you provided that information to reporters in an envelope slipped under the door, your identity would not have been known to them, isn't that right?
>
> A: Yes, I could have secretly gone around and slipped the envelope under the door, but instead I trusted the defendants to keep their word to me.

That turned out to be everybody's favorite question. Appellate judges went on to ask Rothenberg the same question two more times.

But for now, Hannah wound down.

Rothenberg now had the opportunity to rehabilitate me in his redirect examination. During the luncheon recess, I had asked him to erase that damn word, *opprobrium,* from the blackboard so that the jury wouldn't be reminded of it. He dutifully complied. Then he reminded them of it.

Rothenberg launched into a series of questions designed to persuade the jury that I had not been aware of what *opprobrium* meant when I used it during my deposition. As he questioned me, I could see Fitzmaurice over his shoulder. He was barely able to suppress a smirk.

Finally, it was over, and I left the witness stand. For six years, I had been brooding about what they would ask me and how I would respond. There had been no major surprises.

What they *hadn't* asked me seemed more significant. It's *The Hound of the Baskervilles* principle. The key clue was that the dog *didn't* bark. Homicide cops will tell you that their suspicions are aroused when a suspect fails to ask about the details of how the murder was committed. Why don't they ask? They know the answer. They don't want to hear it.

I had learned to listen for the non-bark for years.

Back when my old boss, Pat Fallon, had left Martin/Williams to start his own agency, he raided our shop mercilessly. Every week or so he would call me, checking on the effect his forays were having, and whether or not I thought this art director or that copywriter was happy at Martin/Williams. I'd dance with him and then, forever a slave to the bureaucratic impulse, report the calls to my supervisor, Dave Floren.

After one of these chats with Fallon, I told Floren I thought Fallon had been in touch with John Francis, among our best copywriters.

"How do you know?" asked Floren.

"Because Fallon didn't ask me about him," I said.

Floren found out it was true and upped the ante before Francis accepted Fallon's offer. Francis stayed on board at Martin/Williams.

Back in the courtroom, I continued to listen for the non-bark. Fitzmaurice had not asked me about Edwards, the case that had haunted me for nearly twenty years. It had been the subject of countless memos from me to Hvass and Rothenberg. When I sued the papers, my greatest fear had been that they would reopen the old wounds, expose my weakness, point out the inconsistency of my claims of betrayal.

I had been burned when I trusted the papers not to disclose me as the source of Edwards's record, just as I had been burned when I trusted them not to disclose me as the source of Johnson's record. Why should I have been so upset about it this time? I had been through it all before. I don't know how I would have been able to answer if the defendants had questioned me about Edwards. Why didn't they? Wouldn't they be able to use my Edwards experience to convince the jury that I should have known better than to rely on a reporter's promise of anonymity? Or, to put it more delicately, I should have known promises of confidentiality were conditional.

Although it might have worked, stripped of any pretty packaging, the heart of that argument is "You should have known we are liars." The papers weren't about to admit that. They were claiming that exposing me was highly unusual conduct. How do you sell that notion to a jury if the defendants point out that they had done it to me before?

There was more unexplored territory. Why wasn't I questioned more closely as to why no one else at the Whitney headquarters meeting had agreed to serve as the media contact? Gary Flakne had taken the time to ferret out Johnson's record. He had taken the time to drive me from Whitney's headquarters to the suburbs, where my car was being repaired. Why didn't he have the time to meet with the reporters? And what about Ismach, the journalism professor? He was the person with the title of media consultant, which went with the responsibility for dealing with the media. Why didn't he deliver the goods?

The defense didn't ask those questions because the answers would have shown me for what I really was. Not a shrewd political operative manipulating the press. A fool. An errand boy. The other people at the campaign meeting were savvy enough to realize what was coming down: a high-risk desperation operation. They knew that whoever was handing out these documents might be burned once the press realized we were forcing them to run the story by creating a competitive situation, pitting one paper against the other. None of them wanted their fingerprints on it.

The other question that hadn't been asked was the one I should have asked myself when I walked into that meeting: what was I doing in that room?

There was George Thiss, a top aide to a United States senator; Arnold Ismach, a journalism professor; Gary Flakne, a former county attorney and legislator; and Jerry Olson, a public relations executive with a company listed on the New York Stock Exchange. This was Whitney's kitchen cabinet, his most trusted advisers, his top echelon, the big hitters. They were the strategists, the planners, the brains behind the campaign. I was a latecomer who had an occasional freelance assignment writing first drafts of unread position papers. I'd never been asked to one of these meetings previously. I came because I was hoping to run up a few hours on my time sheet.

Four generals and a private. Guess who volunteers to go over to the state capitol with a bomb strapped to his chest? The only guy they could think of dumb enough to go on a suicide mission for a candidate twenty points down in the polls.

But that doesn't explain why I did it. I wasn't really that dumb. I had never read the psychiatrist's report that Fitzmaurice had mentioned, but he had given me a pretty good idea of what was in it.

"A classic pattern," Fitzmaurice had said. Instead of failing outright, I put myself into situations that were bound to blow up in my face. That way I could blame someone else for my failure.

I had been through the whole drill before with Edwards. There was no logical reason for me to get involved in this latest farce. I didn't care if Marlene Johnson had a minor police record. I wouldn't have recognized her if she had walked into the room. I had no real stake in Whitney's election until the story broke. I didn't dig up the documents. Flakne did. He even had to explain the legal jargon in them to me.

Why didn't he deliver them?

I didn't ask him.

Why not our media consultant, Arnold Ismach?

I didn't ask him, either.

Just point me the way to the front.

I justified my conduct as loyalty. I was loyal to Whitney. Loyal to my agreement to carry out my assignment. Loyal to my decision to punish the press for having lied to me.

But hadn't Whitney lied, too? He must have known what we were doing. At best, he hadn't stuck out his neck for me.

Hadn't Flakne sent me into battle because he was afraid to go himself? Hadn't he ducked when the press called and asked him about the documents?

It didn't really matter to me. I wasn't angry with them. I more or less expected them to act as they had. The weaker they seemed, the more opportunity it gave me to appear strong. Loyal. Determined.

I anointed myself with newly minted virtues.

The psychiatrist had been right. I had followed the classic pattern and failed again. I had been heaped with opprobrium. I was back to where I had been twenty years ago when I had blown the Edwards case. I knew why I was there.

So I could try to rewrite the last act of the Edwards case and finally come out a winner.

CHAPTER SIXTEEN

Who's Who?

We got through our next witness, Gerry Nelson, the AP reporter, with no surprises. Nelson had been the third reporter I'd visited in the warren of offices that were cheek by jowl in the capitol basement. By the time I got to him, what I was doing had become as obvious as if I had stood at the end of the hallway with my envelopes and conducted a mail call.

Nelson testified that it was important to keep promises given to sources, that he had done so, and that he had known he had not gotten the Johnson materials on an exclusive basis.

Hannah couldn't shake him. Fitzmaurice didn't even bother to try, waving him off the stand as if he were shooing away a mosquito.

Earlier, my testimony had been interrupted briefly so that another of our witnesses, Roger Buoen, who was going out of town, could testify out of turn. Buoen was an assistant city editor and Lori Sturdevant's immediate supervisor. He testified that Sturdevant's promise to me should have been honored. Good stuff. Neither Hannah nor Fitzmaurice had cross-examined.

Fitzmaurice didn't panic every time we scored. We'd score some. He'd score some. At one time or another, the sun shines on every dog's ass. Trying to block every shot would be counterproductive. Next.

Rothenberg called Bill Salisbury, the *Pioneer Press* reporter.

His direct testimony matched the description Rothenberg had made in his opening remarks. Salisbury had made the promise. He had not requested exclusivity. When his editors decided to break the promise, he had objected strenuously.

Rothenberg wanted to question Salisbury about articles he had written subsequent to the Johnson incident. They involved charges of corruption made by anonymous sources against legislators.

The judge overruled Hannah's objection to this. We got the article into evidence and Rothenberg made his point. It was a key ruling.

Rothenberg produced another Salisbury article. An anonymous source had predicted that the next chief justice of the Minnesota Supreme Court would be A. M. Keith. The article had appeared a week *after* a nearly identical article in the *Star Tribune* also had quoted an anonymous source who predicted Keith's appointment. Hannah objected. The judge overruled.

It was another key ruling. Now Rothenberg could show that even when there obviously was no exclusivity, the *Pioneer Press* still honored a promise of anonymity. There was no cross-examination.

Rothenberg called Lori Sturdevant as his next witness.

She confirmed his opening statement version of what her testimony would be: the promise. Her knowledge that there would be no exclusivity. The breaking of the promise. Her refusal to have her byline appear on the article.

Rothenberg tried to get in an article Sturdevant had written about Robert Mattson, a candidate for reelection as state treasurer in 1984. Nine days before the primary, the *Star Tribune* disclosed Mattson's considerable financial problems. The information had been furnished by an anonymous source.

Fitzmaurice objected. The court overruled. The article was admitted.

Rothenberg had kicked out three of the legs of the defendants' dirty tricks stool. Other anonymous sources weren't charged with dirty tricks or betrayed when they charged public officials with illegal acts, or furnished their information on a nonexclusive basis, or provided it just a few days before an election. Our case was beginning to build. There was no cross-examination.

The last reporter I gave the documents to was WCCO-TV's Dave Nimmer. Nimmer was my idea, not Ismach's. I had known him since I was an alderman and he was a city hall reporter, fifteen years earlier. For a time, he had been the reporters' guild representative. Later, he became managing editor of the *Star*.

Going from what amounted to being a union rep to the management side of the table was an unusual transition, but Nimmer had unusual political skills. He was a bridge between the pressroom and the front office. He could manage the working stiffs who put out the paper and still relate to the elitist types who ran it and owned it.

Nimmer affected a kind of cynical, but heart-of-gold style that worked well with the pols, reporters, and cops he had to deal with. He had the best cop sources on the paper, including a few generally thought to be on the pad.

Nimmer left the paper and went to television reporting. Long after both of us had left city hall, I was still giving him the occasional news tip. We'd even taken a fishing trip together in northern Minnesota. I trusted Nimmer. Rothenberg went through the usual litany. Nimmer testified that he was aware he didn't have the material on an exclusive basis.

> Q: (by Rothenberg): Okay, Mr. Nimmer, you've been fairly familiar with the case here. I believe you—didn't you appear on a panel at the St. Thomas College a while back discussing this?
> A: (by Nimmer): Yes, I did.
> Q: And you are aware, Mr. Nimmer, that the *Minneapolis Star & Tribune* and the *St. Paul Pioneer Press* did decide to dishonor the promises that their reporters had given to Mr. Cohen?
> A: Yes.
> Q: And how do you feel about that, Mr. Nimmer?

A: I try not to have opinions. What I said at the forum is what I'll repeat here. I said I thought they hung Mr. Cohen out to dry because they didn't regard him very highly as a source.

Good stuff. I was surprised when Fitzmaurice decided to cross-examine.

Q: (by Fitzmaurice): And the reason that you made the recommendation that it not be used at all, was it a judgment that you made that the information about Marlene Johnson was basically old information, dealing with an insignificant or petty thing that had happened long, long ago, in part?

A: The word I remember I used was "chickenshit," sir.

Q: And in your view, in making that recommendation, did you think that publishing the information raw, just straight-out news story, Marlene Johnson convicted of shoplifting 12 years ago, or something to that effect, without identifying the source at all, would have been, in effect, unfair to her?

A: I didn't believe it was fair to the campaign. I thought it was silly.

Q: Would it ... fall within the general category of political dirty trick at the Eleventh Hour in the campaign?

A: The answer would be yes, except that I've seen it happen every campaign I can recall, and it is no worse than most.

So much for our carefully built foundation. Chickenshit? Bullshit. He had never used that word to me in describing my actions. And he had never told me that exclusivity was the rule of thumb, or that my giving him the documents was a dirty trick.

Never. My trusted old city hall fishing buddy had blown me away.

Q: (redirect by Rothenberg): Okay, now Mr. Fitzmaurice referred to the phrase "dirty trick" as he has throughout this trial.

Now Mr. Nimmer, isn't the exposure of a source, a violation of a promise without the source's consent, does not that fall within the category of "dirty trick"?

A: In journalistic terms?
Q: Yes, sir.
A: Yes sir, in my opinion.
MR. ROTHENBERG: Thank you, Mr. Nimmer.

Now I get it. I played a dirty trick. They played a dirty trick. The world-weary reporter casts a dubious eye upon us benighted slobs and passes judgment. We're all bums. Still, there was chickenshit out there along with opprobrium. Pretty thin stuff, but I didn't underestimate Fitzmaurice's ability to make something out of it.

To add to the fun, somewhere along the way, Judge Knoll had gotten his wires crossed and begun referring to "Mr. Rothenberg" as "Mr. Cohen." It had happened at least three times in open court. Each time Judge Knoll had caught himself, and apologized profusely, calling all the more attention to it.

"Lessee now, you're the one from Pinsk and he's the one from Minsk, right? Or are you the one from Minsk and he's the one from Pinsk?"

CHAPTER SEVENTEEN

Tie Ballgame?

Our next witness, Pat Fallon, testified that I had become a pariah in the advertising community and that "if not for the cloud placed over him by these articles in the newspapers," I would be earning "in the low six figures."

It was a pretty generous appraisal, considering that Martin/Williams had just raised me to $36,500 before they fired me. Both Fitzmaurice and Hannah tried to shake him, but couldn't.

Rothenberg called Flakne.

When I had first gotten to know Gary Flakne more than twenty years earlier, he was one of several young Turks who did what young Turks do: take control of the party from the old guard. He served five terms in the state legislature, where he developed a reputation as irreverent, quick-witted, and everyone's—Democrat or Republican—first choice to emcee their fund-raisers. A Republican-controlled county board had appointed him county attorney. He lost the seat to a liberal Democrat six years later and went into private practice. As the years rolled by, the pounds rolled on, and by the time of the trial, the once lean and hungry young Turk had ballooned to much more generous proportions.

Flakne testified about how he had gotten the documents from the office of public records.

> Q: (by Rothenberg): Mr. Flakne, what was Mr. Cohen's attitude about distributing these documents and disseminating

them to the members of the press, as you understand, at that meeting?

A: (by Flakne): Something less than enthusiastic, as was mine. We had in the meeting with George Thiss, George was an old-time, long-time friend who really asked me to do this, pardon me. I had indicated I would do that, but that I really didn't want to get involved in that campaign.

When I came back and said, "Well, here is what I found, now what do you want to do with it," it was pretty obvious to George at that point, and certainly to Dan, that I had done my function. I didn't want to do any more.

By the time of the trial, Thiss had been dead for two years. Fitzmaurice cross-examined.

Q: (by Fitzmaurice): And Mr. Thiss was the same Mr. Thiss who gave you this assignment, as you've called it, to go over and check these records out?

A: That's correct.

Now came another one of those surprises that shouldn't have been such a big surprise. Flakne testified that he and I and Thiss had attended two meetings. The first meeting had taken place *before* he got the documents. Hannah cross-examined:

Q: (by Hannah): Now, the first meeting, as far as you can recollect, had three participants, you, George Thiss, and Dan Cohen; is that right?

A: (by Flakne): That's right. I think I indicated to Mr. Fitzmaurice that there may have been others, but I don't want to testify that that's true, because I can't recollect. Those—the three of us I do remember, specifically.

Q: And the second meeting after—the meeting which occurred subsequent to the time you got the documents from Ramsey County, the participants, as far as you can recollect, are you, Mr. Cohen, and Mr. Thiss.

A: Yes, sir.

I could only guess why Flakne said there had been two meet-ings. There had been only one meeting, at least only one that I knew about or attended, and that took place *after* Flakne had got-ten the documents. Was the late George Thiss being resurrected to perform one last service for the Republican Party: taking the rap for having ordered the hit on Marlene Johnson? If so, why put me there, too?

Flakne was our witness. You don't impeach your own witness.

> Q: (redirect by Rothenberg): Okay, now, Mr. Flakne, as I understand from your answer, it was Mr. Thiss who requested or directed you to obtain these court documents, wasn't it? George Thiss?
>
> A: (by Flakne): He asked—yeah, request, yes.
>
> Q: And it was Mr. Thiss, not Mr. Cohen?
>
> A: No, Mr. Cohen did not ask me to.
>
> Q: Okay. Thank you for—Mr. Flakne, I believe that Mr. Fitzmaurice, in his opening statement, said something to the effect that somehow you were the individual who had provid-ed Mr. Cohen's name to the newspaper. Is that correct?
>
> A: Absolutely not.

Okay, he hadn't given my name to the *Star Tribune*. If he had, the paper could claim they had learned of my identity as the source of the documents independently, and were free to name me without my permission. Why did Fitzmaurice say Flakne had given me up? What did he know that we didn't?

Rothenberg started to rebuild our foundation.

After several minor witnesses, Rothenberg called Doug Hennes, who had been Salisbury's immediate supervisor in October 1982.

Rothenberg asked the usual questions and got the usual answers. Hennes testified that he knew of no other instance where a promise of anonymity to a confidential source had been broken. After the election, the St. Paul papers held a meeting of editors and reporters to do a postmortem on the incident and discuss the paper's policy on confidentiality.

> Q (by Rothenberg): Now, it's true, is it not, according to your own knowledge, that Marlene Johnson, present Lieutenant Governor Marlene Johnson, was, at the time, and continues to be, a good friend of your Editor, Deborah Howell; that's true, is it not?
>
> A (by Hennes): Yes.
>
> Q: Okay. And that was a meeting, I think, as discussed earlier, where many reporters had objected to the decision to violate Mr. Salisbury's promise of confidentiality?
>
> A (by Hennes): Yes, they objected.
>
> Q: And it was a very heated meeting, wasn't it?
>
> A: People expressed their opinion, Dave [Hall] explained why he made the decision, and that was it. I don't know that I would characterize it as heated. People were upset.
>
> Q (Rothenberg reading from Hennes's deposition): Do you recall whether or not anyone expressed the opinion that Cohen should have been identified or was properly identified?
>
> A: Yes.
>
> Q: Who?
>
> A: Well, Ms. Howell.
>
> Q: Okay, so, Mr. Hennes, the only person whom you could recall as supporting the decision to name Mr. Cohen and violate the promise of Mr. Salisbury to Mr. Cohen was the same Ms. Howell who happened to be a personal friend of Marlene Johnson; isn't that correct?
>
> A: Yes.

It was Friday afternoon. The court recessed until Monday.

The pattern for the trial had been set. We would try to show that they had violated a basic tenet of journalism when they revealed my name. They would try to show that their conduct was justified because I had played a dirty trick.

CHAPTER EIGHTEEN

"Oh, Now I Get It!"

On Monday, Arnold Ismach was the only witness. He was on the stand for the entire day. Since the incident, he had become dean of the School of Journalism at the University of Oregon, and he had flown in from Oregon to testify.

Ismach described the meeting with Flakne and me, and then, carrying the best set of journalistic credentials of anyone who testified at the trial, gave a long, scholarly, articulate analysis of the significance of confidential sources to the news business.

He described the shield laws, promoted by newspapers themselves, including these defendants, to prevent judges from holding reporters in contempt of court and sending them to jail for refusing to reveal confidential sources. Applying a little touch of PR, the Minnesota statute was titled "The Free Flow of Information Act." That was supposed to signify its purpose: protecting reporters' sources gave the sources confidence their identities would not be revealed, which would facilitate the free flow of information.

Ismach also read from a couple of killer articles that Fitzmaurice was unable to keep out of evidence.

> Q (by Rothenberg): Is Mr. [Bob] Woodward the man who dealt with Deep Throat?
>
> A (by Ismach): Yes. The Woodward comment that I was referring to in the issue of the Columbia Journalism Review for July–August of '88.

> This isn't simply a matter of just deciding to break a promise, to break a pledge of confidentiality, he, Woodward says, that reporters generally agree to keep a source's identity secret until the source dies or releases the reporter from the promise of confidentiality.
>
> Q: And you mentioned, Dr. Ismach, one or two more illustrations that you'd like to provide.
>
> A: One that struck me upon reading it, Marvin Kalb, who has been a network television correspondent for many years was quoted as saying, about confidentiality, quote, "You can't eat off a source's plate and then later say you don't like the food."

He ended his direct testimony by characterizing the defendants' conduct as "unethical."

For once, Fitzmaurice's cross-examination didn't do much more than reinforce the witness's credibility:

> Q (by Fitzmaurice): Are you being paid for your testimony?
> A (by Ismach): No, I am not.
> Q: You're here, then, as a volunteer?
> A: I was requested to serve as a witness and offered payment, but I refused.

Fitzmaurice did his usual number. He got in some dirty tricks stuff from an article concerning Senator Joseph Biden and an aide to Governor Michael Dukakis. He forced Ismach to admit that he had been ambivalent, at best, about going public with Johnson's record. It didn't amount to much compared to the significance of Ismach's presence at my meeting with Flakne.

Dean Arnold Ismach was not a hired gun, paid to support my position *after* the fact. He had been there on the morning of October 27, 1982. He had drawn up the list of reporters—with one dumb addition from me. He had told me how to word my offer to exchange the documents for anonymity.

I had taken the advice of a world-class journalism expert who had been at my elbow advising me how to cut an ironclad deal with the press. How could I have acted more responsibly?

The defendants had an answer for all of it: it was a dirty trick.

The next day, after a couple of minor witnesses, we called *Star Tribune* columnist Jim Klobuchar for cross-examination under the rules. That permitted us to cross-examine first, as part of our case, to be followed by the defendants' direct examination.

Klobuchar and I had had our ups and downs over the years. When I was still on the city council, a fellow alderman, Mark Anderson, and I had concocted separate baseball dream teams. Mine was the All-Jewish All-Star Team. His was the All-Swedish All-Star Team. We presented our lineups to Klobuchar, the impartial Slavic arbiter, and asked him to declare a winner. After carefully analyzing the slow-footed, largely marginal performers our respective forebears had produced, and eliminating ringers like Walter Johnson (he was of German background, not Swedish), Klobuchar wrote a funny column, concluding correctly that they were about evenly matched and that both teams were so bad neither could win.

The column he produced on the Johnson incident the day after I was fired was something else. He referred to my role as a "sham … sleazy … the shabbiest kind of late thrown kidney punch."

> Q (by Rothenberg): As a matter of fact, not in this article or in any article or in any subsequent article for the next several months did you disclose to your readers any work on behalf of Mr. Perpich, now Governor Perpich, did you, Mr. Klobuchar?
>
> A (by Klobuchar): If I may ask, what was the work that you're referring to?
>
> Q: As a matter of fact … you actually helped write his inaugural speech; isn't that true?
>
> A: That was material that I helped—that I provided to Mr. Perpich, and that was two months after this election. …

Q: And it was disclosed January 4th, 1983, 15 days later, in a column, not in a column, but in an article, whose author is unnamed, by—entitled "Klobuchar Helped Write Perpich Inaugural Speech." In other words, disclosed by another writer and not by yourself; is that right?

A: The request by Mr. Perpich for some assistance, some, ideas in connection with his inaugural was made in a meeting in December, and the actual writing was done ten days later or something like that, so it was very close to the time.

The article, which was introduced in evidence, read:

> Managing editor news, Frank Wright, said yesterday, "Klobuchar's participation in this came to the attention of *Star & Tribune* editors today, and editors have raised concerns about possible conflicts of interest on the ground that Klobuchar has written periodically about Rudy and other matters of state government. At this point, we have the matter under review."
>
> Klobuchar declined to comment.

The paper gave him a five-day suspension.

Q: Okay. Now Mr. Klobuchar, you also refer [in his article about Cohen's part in the Johnson incident] to a quotation by Mr. Cohen, refer quite frequently to a comment about something to the effect of living a lie?

A: Yes, I made that reference.

Q: Now, Mr. Klobuchar, you, in nowhere in that article refer to … that first sentence in Mr. Cohen's quotation ["The voters of this state are entitled to know that kind of information"], do you, sir?

A: I did not.

Q: Okay. And do you feel, Mr. Klobuchar, that it's important to quote sources properly?

A: I think it is, yes.

Q: It's true, is it not, Mr. Klobuchar, that a few months before the article appeared on Mr. Cohen, which you have before you,

you were suspended by the *Minneapolis Star & Tribune* for quoting a source inaccurately; isn't that true?

A: Yes.

MR. ROTHENBERG: No further questions.

He was suspended for five days that time, too. He had made up a quote in a column he wrote about the Minnesota Vikings football team.

In his direct, Fitzmaurice asked Klobuchar about his background. Like Perpich, Klobuchar was the son of eastern European immigrants and had grown up on Minnesota's Iron Range. Fitzmaurice questioned him about a column he had written before the incident "relative to Mr. Perpich's decision to enter the race for the position of Governor in this state."

> A (by Klobuchar): It's a column I wrote based on a conversation I had with Rudy Perpich the day before.
>
> Q (by Fitzmaurice): You used the phrase in that column that you write, the "arms-length relationship" between columnists or reporters and journalists and politicians. What did you mean by that, sir?
>
> A: That journalists are traditionally supposed not to be on socially good terms with people who are potentially sources of theirs. But it is very difficult over a period of time for journalists not to be, to develop friendly relationships with people they cover, with some people they cover, and in the case of Perpich, we had the same roots, our parents came from the same part of the world, it was a kind of kinship, a blood tie, and I was trying to acknowledge that and also at the same time that the journalist has to be, where he or she can and must, detached.

"In the case of Perpich" there were "roots, our parents came from the same part of the world ... kinship, a blood tie."

In the case of Cohen, however, there were no roots. Our parents had not come from the same part of the world. There was no kinship. He and I had no blood tie.

Klobuchar's explanation of how he felt about Perpich also said, without saying anything, something about how he felt about me.

Something else also had gone unmentioned. In his October 29 column, Klobuchar hadn't mentioned my having provided the documents as an anonymous source. Perpich's confidential speechwriter—who had testified he hadn't surreptitiously helped Perpich with his speeches until after the 1982 election—never criticized me for providing the documents confidentially. Nonbow-nonwow.

Rothenberg called Doug Grow next. Grow had written a column three weeks after I was fired criticizing the University of Minnesota athletic department for giving me a freelance writing assignment. Fred Konrath, one of the recruiters, had testified that Grow had asked him why the U of M would want to "use a person like Dan" to write football recruiting brochures.

Rothenberg cross-examined under the rules.

> Q (by Rothenberg): Mr. Grow, who tipped you off to Mr. Cohen's employment by the University of Minnesota?
>
> A (by Grow): A source.
>
> Q: All right. In other words, this is a source which you promised confidentiality to?
>
> A: Yes.
>
> Q: And you have kept that promise of confidentiality to the source until this very day?
>
> A: And I still will.
>
> Q: You still will, and I certainly would not want to ask you to divulge the name of that source. Your promise should be honored. In that case, did your editors approve your promise of confidentiality to that source?
>
> A: We didn't discuss it.
>
> Q: You did not discuss it with your editors?
>
> A: No.
>
> Q: Okay. So it's something where you, as an individual, without approval of your editors, were able to give a promise of con-

fidentiality to a source and the editors did not dishonor that promise?

A: What I—I'd like to point out I did not use the source for the story. That was just the lead to the story.

Q: But you said ... something to the effect that it did not make sense that the University would hire somebody like Cohen who was unpopular with the administration just elected, that it was a politically unwise thing to do, it was inexpedient, those were the words you used, didn't you?

A: Yes, on Mr. Giel's [the University's men's athletic director] part, yes, sir.

Q: Mr. Giel said that.

A: No, I said on Mr. Giel's part. I'm sorry.

Q: It was—all right. It was inexpedient for Mr. Giel to hire Mr. Cohen?

A: It seemed—it did seem, yes, sir.

Q: And of course it wouldn't have been limited to Mr. Giel; that same inexpediency that you talk about, incidentally, several weeks after the event, would apply to other possible employers too, you could say the same thing about Mr. Jones from this company or Mr. Smith from this government agency?

A: If that's a question, the difference is quite distinct, to me. Those are not institutions that are involved in the political arena, in the public arena.

Q: Well, I mentioned state agencies, sir. This would apply—

A: Okay, I thought Mr. Jones was private. Okay. ... No, I would think that it would be very unwise for the head of the PCA [Pollution Control Agency], for example, at that point, to hire Mr. Cohen to do public relations work.

Q: So then it would be unwise, then, for the employer in any public agency, the University or the PCA or any other public agency to take on Mr. Cohen?

A: At that point, yes, sir.

Q: I see. And even though Mr. Cohen is performing good work for whoever he's working for?

A: As I understand it, that's part of the spoils system of the American political system, yes, sir.

Q: We have a situation then, when Mr. Cohen is out of work, where Ms. Johnson has been elected [Lieutenant] Governor, Mr. Cohen obviously has to find some work to feed his family. When is it going to be expedient for Mr. Cohen, Mr. Grow, for employers to employ him and allow him to feed his family? How many months? How many days? How many weeks? How many years are we going to have to wait?

A: I would—

Q: Six years after?

A: What usually happens, as I understand it, in the political system, is that when the—when your party comes to power that usually is good times for you. When your party's out of power, you usually have a private job.

Q: And as a matter of fact, one of the effects of your article could be, would it not, Mr. Grow, that … this article would discourage other public agencies from giving Mr. Cohen work on the grounds that it would not be quote, "expedient," unquote, to do so.

A: I don't know.

MR. ROTHENBERG: Thank you, Mr. Grow.

Okay, now I see where I went wrong. Klobuchar: wrong blood. Grow: wrong party.

CHAPTER NINETEEN

From Comedy to Film Noir

The next day, Rothenberg called Sid Hartman, the most popular sports commentator in the state. Hartman wrote a column in the *Star Tribune* and also did a daily report and a Sunday morning show on WCCO-AM, Minnesota's highest-rated radio station.

> Q (by Rothenberg): Mr. Hartman, the record, what is your position—
>
> THE COURT: Not Sidney, just Sid?
>
> THE WITNESS: Sid.
>
> THE COURT: All right. Go ahead.
>
> Q (by Rothenberg): What is your position with the *Star & Tribune*?
>
> A: I'm a columnist and I have a title of Sports Editor.
>
> Q: And how long have you been the Sports Editor?
>
> A: I've been with the paper close to 40 years.
>
> THE COURT: I should point out, I can't resist this. I swept the seats, under the seats in Nicollet Park, and in the Met Center, and I think I met you when I was sweeping under the seats at the park. Because once in a while we were allowed to enter the press box.
>
> THE WITNESS: I see.
>
> THE COURT: That was about 70 years ago.
>
> THE WITNESS: Long time.
>
> THE COURT: That's the comic relief for the day. Go ahead.

Sid said "confidential sources are important" and cast his aura of celebrityhood over the courtroom. Fitzmaurice and Hannah both passed.

If the Sidster was comic relief, the next witness, Lou Gelfand, was film noir.

On November 7, 1982, the Sunday after the election, Gelfand, the *Star Tribune's* readers' representative, had written a column arguing that the paper was free to break a promise of confidentiality to me because I had violated the "unspoken standard of journalism that defines the substance of Cohen's tip as beneath the threshold of acceptable, unattributable information." He wrote a second column on November 21 that seemed to back off a little from the first. After quoting several of the comments he had received, pro and con, on his November 7 column, he wrote:

> Comment: The confrontation is based on different perceptions of what constitutes a confidence. The perception comes from equally honest and honorable bases.

> I've concluded that Cohen because of his 20-year relationship with the media, must have shared some of the editors' perceptions of what constitutes a confidence; that the editorial assumption of Cohen's news media know-how was a strong factor in their decision

And this mildest of rebukes to his employer:

> The Oct. 28 article should have included an explanation of the confidentiality Cohen was promised and why it was not honored.

What was clear from this comment, written in the somewhat murky and convoluted style of a PR guy trying to inch away from a previous comment, was that he had overreached in his earlier column and was having second thoughts.

Professionally, Gelfand was in an unenviable position. He'd been a reporter for the St. Paul paper for nine years, but that was a quarter of a century prior to when he had become the readers' representative.

During the previous twenty-five years, he'd been a PR guy, five years with a railroad, three years with the Guthrie Theater, and seventeen years with Pillsbury. He'd been the readers' representative for just a year prior to the Johnson incident.

Lots of newsies become PR types. The money's much better, and it's a lot less stressful. But once you jump ship from the newsroom into the corporate world, the hatch slams behind you. To a true blue newsie, you have sold out.

Gelfand made the jump back, but to the guys he passed in the hall every day, he had a lot to prove.

Gelfand's more sophisticated readers, the news junkies, the public equivalent of the newsies, also tended to be skeptical. The paper could call Gelfand the readers' representative, but it was John Cowles Jr.—or the Cowles corporate treasurer—who signed his paycheck.

Gelfand was attempting to straddle two worlds in an even more fundamental way. A Gelfand had not always been a Gelfand. Sometime in the past the name had been Garfinkel. It must not have been easy for him, particularly at a place like Pillsbury and in an industry like flour milling, where Garfinkels were few and far between.

Gelfand was the first witness who had sat in on the October 28 huddle, the daily, late afternoon meeting of the *Star Tribune's* news editors in which they discussed how the paper would handle the major stories of the day. He had an insider's knowledge of how the decision had been made to dishonor the promise to me.

Rothenberg wheeled out the heavy artillery. He intended to use every weapon in our arsenal to impeach Gelfand's credibility.

Gelfand unwittingly contributed to that strategy. The way witnesses respond to cross-examination more or less resembles parenting styles when the parent is trying to say no. There's the Maybe-We'll-Do-It-Someday-but-Not-Now type. Of all the *Star Tribune* witnesses, Tim McGuire was by far the master of this genre, seeming to concede the reasonableness of whatever point we were trying to make, while utterly denying its application in our case. Then there are the calm but firm naysayers, like Frank Wright, who wrap their motivations in the moral probity of What's-Best-for-the-Entire-Known-World. Hardliners like Klobuchar, Grow, and Gelfand make the weakest witnesses because they are unwilling to concede validity to any view but their own. They're the No-Means-No-and-That's-That types. They don't like to have their decisions questioned, and it shows—to a jury.

To begin his questioning of Gelfand, Rothenberg placed a *Star Tribune* editorial cartoon into evidence. It showed a police lineup of young women in bathing suits. The sashes across their chests read "Miss Indiana," "Miss North Dakota," Miss Iowa," and, instead of "Miss Minnesota," "Miss Demeanor." Earlier, it had been revealed—and the *Star Tribune* had reported—that the Miss Minnesota contestant had been convicted of shoplifting as a teenager. She was forced to resign as Miss Minnesota USA.

> Q (by Rothenberg): Mr. Gelfand, may I ask your opinion of the cartoon just shown you which has a picture in the cartoon by a gentleman named Sack. "Miss Indiana. Miss North Dakota. Miss Iowa. Miss Demeanor," with a jail ball attached to her, all dressed as Miss America candidates. What do you think of that cartoon? Was it appropriate for the *Star & Tribune* to run that cartoon, sir?
>
> A: Well, in terms of the purposes intended, it was very good.
>
> Q: It was very good at making fun of a young lady who had been convicted of shoplifting when she was 16 years old?
>
> A: Right. It did, and that's what it was intended to do.
>
> Q: So then, Mr. Gelfand, it is appropriate and indeed a matter of reader interest to have an editorial cartoon, a long article starting on page 1B, a headline on page 1A about a past conviction of shoplifting of a Miss Minnesota USA candidate, a past conviction when she was a teenager, that's appropriate, you say?
>
> A: The news and editorial department at the *Star & Tribune* are separate; they're independent of one another, and I wouldn't

have, under any conditions, written anything about the drawing because that's not my accountability, but I would say that it was a cartoon, used exaggeration with skill, that there was a high reader interest in it. Yes, I thought the cartoon was outstanding. … Whether I agree with it or not is not the issue, but in terms of meeting the test of an outstanding drawing, that it was.

Q: Okay. Then, Mr. Gelfand, you're saying then, that it's appropriate to give extensive coverage and an editorial cartoon to a Miss Minnesota USA candidate for a beauty contest for something which happened to her earlier when she was a teenager, that's relevant to the public, that's information that the public should know about, but that a similar situation would not apply for a lady who happened to be a candidate for the second highest office in the State of Minnesota, that's trivial, isn't it, Mr. Gelfand?

A: I don't agree with the premise of your question, Counsel. I think they are two totally different situations, and each must be judged on the basis of its own facts in the case, and to try to make a comparison, I don't think is fair.

Q: Okay. Thank you, Mr. Gelfand. … All right. Now, Mr. Gelfand, let's go to the—towards the end of your [November 7] column, okay? It says:

Publishing Cohen's name without his permission is justified by an unspoken standard of journalism that defines the substance of Cohen's tip as beneath the threshold of acceptable, unattributable information.

That's what you wrote?

A: Yes sir.

Q: All right. Now, Mr. Gelfand, you say this is an unspoken standard of journalism. Is it written somewhere? Is it written on tablets? Floating in the courtroom? Do we know what it is? Do we have any idea of what this unspoken standard of journalism is?

A: No, sir, we do not.

Q: Mr. Gelfand, if I were to represent to you that the *Star & Tribune* of May 14th, 1988, three days before another election, ran an article entitled "Candidate Was Accused of Sexual Harassment," a charge that the article later pointed out apparently was dropped. Do you find that to be below your threshold of unattributable information?

A: I find the story acceptable, Counsel.

Q: And, Mr. Gelfand, you find this story acceptable even though it appeared three days before an election, and even though it referred to a sex harassment charge going back to 1983, which—

THE COURT: Mr. Rothenberg, I'm going to sustain an objection that that is repetitive and cumulative. I'm not going to permit that line of questioning.

THE WITNESS: If this had occurred the day before and the man did not have an opportunity to respond, I believe it would have been—the editor should not have used it. The man was given an opportunity to respond, he was running for public office, the information came from court records. I find it appropriate.

Q (by Rothenberg): And that is precisely—and Mr. Gelfand, that is exactly what happened in the case of Marlene Johnson, only the information was not provided one day or three days before, but approximately six or seven days before, also from court records; isn't that correct?

A: That's a correct statement.

Q: And as a matter of fact, Mr. Gelfand, if I would represent to you that you have been a proponent of public disclosure of the names of persons who commit crimes regardless of their personal circumstances, regardless of the humiliating effect on them, that publishing the names of adults guilty of committing crime is appropriate and avoiding publication of their names because of individual circumstances would be unrealistic and impossible to administer, if I were to represent that to you as you having written that May 30, 1982, a few months before the events which are at the heart of this lawsuit, would you agree to that, sir?

A: I think the news media should treat everyone equally.

Q: Fine. And if it prints the names of lowly persons who are convicted of shoplifting, then it should convict—it should publish the names of powerful persons who are also convicted of shoplifting; isn't that correct?

A: No, sir, that's not correct.

Q: Would you say "we should treat everybody equally" is not correct?

A: Generically speaking, I certainly do. But as I said a moment ago, no two cases are the same. If a public figure is charged and convicted of shoplifting, that's different than someone who is not a public figure and is generally unknown.

Q: So that would argue more in favor of identifying the public figure rather than the unknown figure, wouldn't it?

A: It does.

MR. ROTHENBERG: Thank you, Mr. Gelfand.

THE COURT: We'll recess until tomorrow morning.

CHAPTER TWENTY

Forked

The next day, when it was his turn, Fitzmaurice seemed to be treading water. He went over Gelfand's educational and professional background again. He had Gelfand describe, in the most general terms, what it was exactly that took place in a huddle, the daily give-and-take among newspaper senior editors over the content of the next day's paper. Then it was showtime. The courtroom was dimmed. An overhead projector cast the image of Gelfand's November 7 column on a large screen visible to everyone in the courtroom. Waving around a pointer and flipping his half-glasses off and on, Professor Fitzmaurice went through it paragraph by paragraph.

Gelfand again limply explained that my violation of the "unspoken standard of journalism" and my "beneath the threshold" information were only his opinion. Regarding the Miss Minnesota shoplifting cartoon, "No two situations are the same." We'd heard it before.

Rothenberg re-cross-examined. One by one, Rothenberg thrust a half-dozen articles under Gelfand's nose, drawing comparisons from each of them to the Marlene Johnson incident.

What made the information in these articles acceptable, so that promises of anonymity were honored, when the promise to the plaintiff had been dishonored?

One by one, Gelfand parried Rothenberg's attempts at comparison. They were all acceptable. Only the information about Marlene Johnson was not.

As Rothenberg kept hauling out more examples, the cumulative impact of Gelfand's denials began to take on an air of unreality.

It was acceptable to protect the source of the information about Miss Minnesota USA's shoplifting conviction as a sixteen-year-old, because, unlike with Marlene Johnson, the charge against Miss Minnesota USA had not been vacated.

It was acceptable to protect the source who disclosed Bess Myerson's shoplifting conviction, which had occurred eighteen years earlier, because Myerson was a "public figure" and subsequently had been charged with a felony.

It was acceptable to protect the source who furnished information about Senator Biden's plagiarism because Biden had "presidential aspirations."

It was acceptable to protect the source who had furnished information about Judge Ginsberg's alleged marijuana use because marijuana use was "much more serious" than shoplifting.

It was acceptable to protect the source of the information about Fred Isaacs's conviction because it was a "statement of fact."

It was acceptable to disclose a sexual harassment charge three days before an election because the candidate "was given an opportunity to respond."

The more Rothenberg forced Gelfand to make distinctions between these cases and the Johnson case, the less credible Gelfand's answers became.

As Rothenberg gained experience with the introduction of this material, his confidence grew. His voice dripped with sarcasm as Gelfand struggled to justify each new example of acceptability.

Finally, the court had had enough.

> MR. FITZMAURICE: Objected to as repetitious.
> THE COURT: Sustained.

It must have come as a relief to Gelfand when he was no longer being asked to defend the statements in his November 7, 1982, column about "unspoken standards" and "thresholds of acceptable, unattributable information." He had had second thoughts about what he had written two weeks after he wrote it.

Rothenberg went on to a new subject.

> Q: Let's ... continue on the issue of exclusivity. Are you saying that if your newspaper, the *Star Tribune*, had the story about Marlene Johnson's shoplifting conviction on an exclusive basis, that the *Pioneer Press* ... did not have the story, WCCO did not have the story, the Associated Press did not have the story, but that your newspaper would have that story on an exclusive basis, are you saying that then the newspaper should have honored its promise to Mr. Cohen?

Here was Gelfand's chance to cast "unspoken standards" and "thresholds of acceptability" overboard once and for all. He had been troubled about that language anyway. His defense of it against Rothenberg's attacks had not gone terribly well. Rothenberg had offered him a choice, a chance to shift from the shaky soil of "unspoken standards" that were "beneath the threshold" to the firmer ground of exclusivity. The exclusivity argument was still largely intact.

Gelfand/Garfinkel, the newsie/PR guy, was used to jumping from one lily pad to the next. He had done it successfully many times.

He took the leap.

> A: I would have been inclined to have done so.
>
> Q: All right. So then the issue, the real issue we're talking about here, ... Mr. Gelfand, is the issue of commercial advantage to a newspaper ... not the issue of a campaign dirty trick as has been charged by your counsel? The only issue we're talking about, the only reason justifying your newspaper's identification of Mr. Cohen, was not any moral reason, not any ethical reason, but merely the fact that you did not have that informa-

tion on an exclusive basis and that you did not have a scoop on your opposing newspapers?

A: Can't simplify it that well, Counsel. The other issues remained, but I would … have been inclined to have gone ahead and used the story without the source if I had it exclusively. That's my—that's my hypothetical answer.

In chess, there's a situation called a fork. A player maneuvers so as to place not one, but two of his opponent's pieces under simultaneous attack. Rothenberg had forked Gelfand.

Here's a hypothetical situation, Mr. Gelfand. Tell me how you would choose. Assume Cohen had given you the stuff exclusively. Do you burn him or do you not burn him?

Choice one: If you do burn him, you've lost your exclusivity piece. You can't claim you were motivated to disclose his identity because he had taken the "highly unusual … certainly controversial" action of furnishing the documents to more than one news outlet if, when he does give them to you on an exclusive basis, you would burn him anyway.

Choice two: If you don't burn him, you've lost your unspoken standard/dirty trick piece. You can't claim you were motivated to burn him because his behavior was "beneath the threshold of acceptable, unattributable behavior" when you're willing to protect him if you get the fruits of his dirty trick on an exclusive basis.

Rothenberg had given Gelfand a choice. Gelfand chose the second option. He didn't have to choose either option. He could have done what he should have done.

Gelfand could have said, "I don't know," or "I don't understand the question," or, "Both exclusivity and maintaining the highest moral standards are very, very important. I can't choose. And besides, I can't answer a hypothetical question. There are too many other factors that have to be considered."

However, the only choice an opposing counsel will ever offer a witness by way of a hypothetical question is "Heads I win. Tails you lose."

But finally, we had the truth. There was no "unspoken standard." They burned me because they didn't have the material on an exclusive basis. And they didn't have a right to it on an exclusive basis, because that was never part of our deal.

Hoofuckingray.

We'd proved it to ourselves. Having the jury buy it was something else.

CHAPTER TWENTY-ONE

Unforked

Our next two witnesses testified on damages. My accountant trotted out my tax returns. An old friend and client, Dave Printy, a financial consultant, then miraculously transformed my meager income into an enormous loss of pension and retirement benefits.

Printy was not only an expert in his field, he knew how to make a pitch. He festooned the courtroom with graphs, charts, and overlays.

Fitzmaurice cross-examined.

With the accountant, Fitzmaurice had tried to make the income I'd received since I left Martin/Williams seem larger in order to make my damages seem smaller. However, with Printy he had to make the projections of my future income seem smaller, in order to reduce the alleged amount of my lost future benefits from Martin/Williams.

It was confusing, and not too successful. He seemed somewhat surprised by Printy's polished presentation and how well he handled himself under cross-examination.

Fitzmaurice was not one to ignore the impact of Printy's glitzy visuals. He took a magic marker and began writing his own numbers over Printy's, as if he were scribbling graffiti on a political opponent's campaign poster.

> MR. ROTHENBERG: Excuse me, Your Honor, I would object to defacing the exhibit which has already been entered into—and accepted by the Court. If he wants to put up another sheet of paper, that's fine.

THE COURT: I think that's fair enough, Counsel.

MR. FITZMAURICE: Okay, I don't want to deface anything.

THE COURT: Could I—let me just sort of—sorry for the interruption. Cindy, would you get those dried-up markers, take them away from there? These are some that [don't] work, and you just can't see them. Plus, the squeaking is very hard on my inner ear. Throw those old ones out.

Artfully done, but nonetheless, Judge Knoll had taken Fitzmaurice's coloring toys away.

It was a nice moment.

Mike Finney testified next. He was the assistant managing editor of news and had been at the *Star Tribune* only about a year before the incident. Finney had made the initial decision to name me in the article.

Of all the witnesses we deposed, Finney had been the most unpleasant and arrogant. By the time he reached the witness stand, he had been briefed about his demeanor. Watching Finney turn on the charm was like watching Rodney Dangerfield attempt the seduction of Margaret Thatcher. The only thing Finney had ever tried to charm was a T-bone steak, and from the looks of him, he had charmed quite a few of those. He must have been told that his testimony would be better received if he made eye contact with the jury. Every answer wound up with his fond gaze toward the jury box. The jurors began to squirm at his attention.

On October 10, two weeks before the incident, Finney had been quoted in a Gelfand column regarding revelations about public officials in the newspaper:

> This is difficult on the accused, but when a person assumes a public trust, an alleged violation of that trust is news. It should be reported immediately and a paper's obligation is to be fair and thorough. A person accepting a public trust should be subjected to this high degree of scrutiny, but the accused has pro-

tection against any publication that maliciously damages him. The person can bring suit.

> Q (by Rothenberg, cross-examining under the rules): Do you remember that comment?
> A (by Finney): Yes, I do.
> Q: And indeed, that scrutiny had not been given in the case of public figure Marlene Johnson, had it?
> A: If your point is that the shoplifting offense had not been published, you're correct.
> Q: And that's relevant information that the public should know about, isn't it?
> A: Yes.

Finney had been briefed on more than body language. After Gelfand's tussle with exclusivity, Finney obviously had been given some pointers on how to handle the issue.

> Q: All right. Now, Mr. Finney, if you had the information from Mr. Cohen on an exclusive basis, would you then have made the decision to honor the promise to him?
> A: I don't believe that exclusivity is the heart of—exclusivity was not the heart of the decision.

No exclusivity? Rothenberg tried to skewer him with the other prong of the fork.

> Q: All right. Exclusivity was not the heart of the decision… therefore, the arguments made by your newspaper, by the newspapers in this case that the lack of exclusivity somehow was a factor justifying the decision to dishonor the promise made to Mr. Cohen, that then is an error. In fact, exclusivity does not—
> A: It was a factor. For me, it was not a key factor.

Lesson in trial tactics: never try the identical tactic twice in the same trial.

Finney escaped unforked. There was no direct examination.

We moved nearer to the top of the *Star Tribune* food chain. Rothenberg called Joel Kramer for cross-examination. Kramer had been the executive editor of the *Star Tribune* since March 1983. Kramer was McGuire's boss, who was Wright's boss, who was Finney's boss, who was Buoen's boss, who was Sturdevant's boss. For a bunch of liberals, the newspaper hierarchy shaded the court of Louis XIV. Kramer had not been with the paper at the time of the incident. In October 1982, McGuire's boss as editor was Charles Bailey, who was a short-termer at the time; he had resigned to return to Washington. Bailey's boss was the publisher, Donald Dwight, who was fired a few days later, though there was no connection with the incident.

Rothenberg had gotten hold of a tape of a meeting Kramer had attended of investigative reporters and editors from all over the country in June, just a few weeks before the trial. Kramer had appeared on a panel, and though he had said he was not going to answer questions about the case, some members of his audience had pushed the envelope.

> Q (by Rothenberg): The question [quoting one of the questions Kramer had been asked at the meeting] is as follows:
> Do you inform reporters that you can unilaterally revoke promises of confidentiality?
> Answer [by Kramer at the meeting]: I have never done that. I hope that my solution would be not to run the story. I hope that I would have the courage not to run the story.

> Q (by Rothenberg): Did you say that at the meeting, sir?
> A (by Kramer): I could have said it. I recall saying in answer to a question, yes.

The executive editor of the *Minneapolis Star Tribune* had stated his personal alternative to running the story with my name in it—if you had courage, you just didn't run it at all. Nice.

Kramer also admitted that the *Star Tribune* had edited a couple of paragraphs out of a *New York Times* story about Joe Biden in which the editor of the *Des Moines Register* was quoted as saying, "My position is I do not comment on our sources to whom we have granted any degree of anonymity, and regardless of what anyone else might say, we hold to promises of confidentiality."

And Craig R. Whitney, Washington bureau chief for the *New York Times*, said, "We don't discuss our sources."

> Q (by Rothenberg): And you also pointed out in that session that there is a distinction between a source making a comment or an accusation and a source merely providing documents; did you make that distinction?
> A: Yes.

Fitzmaurice couldn't do much with Kramer on direct, except get him to say the quote about courage had been taken out of context.

Fitzmaurice didn't touch the vanished quotes from the *Register* and *Times* editors. How could he? Not only were they in direct contradiction to the practices the *Star Tribune* had followed in my case, but they hadn't appeared in the *Star Tribune* version of the story. We hadn't actually accused them of purposely deleting the quotes in order to avoid having us see them. Still, why not? It wasn't very likely we would stumble across them in the original *Times* version, though that's exactly what happened.

Of course, Kramer could have testified that the *Star Tribune* deleted the quotes to save space, but the denial probably would have backfired, reinforcing whatever suspicions the jurors might have had that the paper's real motive was to keep us from seeing the quotes. So Fitzmaurice chose the least damaging response: he ignored the whole thing.

Once again, the dog didn't bark.

CHAPTER TWENTY-TWO

Our Best Witness

After Kramer stepped down, we moved back to the middle of the *Star Tribune's* hierarchy. Frank Wright was Mike Finney's boss. I'd known Wright for nearly twenty-five years. He was a reporter when I was on the city council. He was head of the *Tribune's* Washington bureau during the brief time I was a bureaucrat with the Peace Corps, and he subsequently became the *Tribune's* foreign correspondent. When we were both in Washington, Frank had written a not-exactly-Watergate non-story about my having fired some Democratic holdovers in the Peace Corps. As a witness, Wright was a polished version of Finney. He spoke directly to the jurors but, unlike Finney, he didn't try to jump into the jury box and hold hands. Rothenberg tried a new approach. If Marlene Johnson were going to be cast in the role of the female as victim, why not Sturdevant, too? Rothenberg cross-examined.

> Q (by Rothenberg): All right. Now, Mr. Wright, you say that you made the final decision on the part of the newspaper to break Ms. Sturdevant's promise to him and identify Mr. Cohen. The buck stopped with you, did it not?
>
> A (by Wright): I made the final decision to publish a story which would reveal the nature of the court action against Marlene Johnson, and also to disclose the source from which that information came.
>
> Q: A decision which, again, was opposed by Ms. Sturdevant, Lori Sturdevant?
>
> A: That was my understanding, yes, in terms of disclosing the source of the information.

143

Q: Then, Mr. Wright, you had been to war-torn areas, been to hot spots of the globe making this coverage. Could you have had the courage to contact Mr. Cohen by yourself instead of sending Lori Sturdevant who opposed that decision considerably to do the dirty work?

A: I'm not sure that was a matter of courage, counsel. She was the reporter working on the story and it seemed appropriate to have her, during the course of the evening, as she did, call him back at least once and perhaps twice to ask if he would relieve her from the—her promise of confidentiality.

Q: And you sent her, the lady who got—who made the promise to Mr. Cohen, the lady who had her promise broken by the editors, to inform Mr. Cohen, rather than you or Mr. Finney who made the decision of breaking that promise, correct?

A: I'm not sure the fact that she was a lady had anything to do with it. The fact that she was a reporter working on the story made it seem appropriate that she would be the one who was in contact with Mr. Cohen.

Our attempt to pose as defenders of American womanhood had fallen flat. We seemed to have run out of ideas, good ideas, anyway. Our testimony had gotten repetitious. The jury was getting restless. But Rothenberg wasn't ready to let go yet. He decided to change topics and focus on the next witness, Ron Clark.

Clark was the editorial editor of the *St. Paul Pioneer Press*. His boss, John Finnegan, was also subpoenaed to testify. Clark had written the "Relevant Disclosures" editorial, which had appeared on Friday, October 29, two days after the Minneapolis and St. Paul papers had written the news articles exposing me. The editorial had said, "Too much is being made … about Republican fingerprints. … The last minute disclosure could have been avoided" if Perpich and Johnson had been forthcoming.

Q (by Rothenberg): Did you approve that editorial, and are you saying that Mr. Finnegan did not veto, he in effect approved that editorial as well?

Wheelock Whitney, the Independent Republican candidate (that's Minnesotan for "Republican") for governor in 1982

Photo by the *Minneapolis Tribune*, courtesy of the Minnesota Historical Society

Rudy Perpich, the DFL candidate (that's Minnesotan for "Democrat") for governor in 1982

Courtesy of the Minnesota Historical Society

"And you think you have trouble with the press?" Face time with Nixon.

Courtesy of the author; photograph taken by White House photographer

Elliot Rothenberg, counsel for the plaintiff

Courtesy of the Minnesota Historical Society

James Fitzmaurice, counsel for the Minneapolis Star Tribune

Courtesy of Faegre & Benson

Bill Salisbury, Capitol Hill Reporter for the St. Paul Pioneer Press

Courtesy of Bill Salisbury

Gary Flakne, former legislator, Hennepin County district attorney, and key adviser to the Whitney campaign

Photo by Zintsmater's Studios, courtesy of the Minnesota Historical Society

Franklin P. Knoll served as a district court judge in Minnesota for eighteen years.

Courtesy of the Minnesota Historical Society

Arnold Ismach, former dean of the Department of Journalism and Communication at the University of Oregon

Courtesy of Arnold Ismach

Bernard Casserly, the plaintiff's expert witness

Courtesy of Bernard Casserly

Marlene Johnson is sworn in as Minnesota's first female lieutenant governor in January 1983.

Courtesy of the Minnesota Historical Society

Rothenberg in front of the Supreme Court building before the oral aruguments in Cohen v. Cowles Media

Courtesy of Special Collections Department, Harvard Law School Library, Modern Manuscript Collection, Elliot Rothenberg Case Files, March 27, 1991, Paige Box 5. Photograph taken by Sarah Rothenberg.

Rothenberg fields questions from members of the press stationed outside the Supreme Court building after the oral arguments.

Courtesy of Special Collections Department, Harvard Law School Library, Modern Manuscript Collection, Elliot Rothenberg Case Files, March 27, 1991, Paige Box 5. Photograph taken by Sarah Rothenberg.

The U.S. Supreme Court justices who decided Cohen v. Cowles Media*: (seated, from left to right) Harry Blackmun, Byron White, William Rehnquist, Thurgood Marshall, and John Paul Stevens; (standing, from left to right) Anthony Kennedy, Sandra Day O'Connor, Antonin Scalia, and David Souter. Rehnquist, Scalia, Kennedy, White, and Stevens decided in favor of Cohen, while O'Connor, Marshall, Blackmun, and Souter sided with the newspapers.*

Collection, the Supreme Court Historical Society. Photographed by Joseph H. Bailey, National Geographic Society.

Dan Cohen shortly after learning the Supreme Court's verdict in June 1991

Photograph by Steve Woit

A (by Clark):Yes.

Q: So that editorial, then, sir, became the position of the *St. Paul Pioneer Press*, did it not?

A:That's the editorial position of the paper, yes.

During cross-examination of Clark, Hannah established that while Finnegan may not have vetoed the editorial, he may not have actually signed off on it, either. Both sides were positioning themselves for Finnegan's future testimony.

Until that time, we were about to rest our case, at least provisionally. But you can't close the show without an expert.

Our expert, Bernie Casserly, had spent fifty years as a working journalist. Casserly was an international figure among journalists specializing in issues of interest to Catholic readers. For twenty-five years, until his retirement in 1982, he had been editor of the *Catholic Bulletin*, the publication of the St. Paul archdiocese. He continued to write a column that was syndicated in Catholic newspapers throughout this country and Ireland. He also wrote a column for the monthly Knights of Columbus magazine, with a million-and-a-half circulation.

Like many people in retirement or semi-retirement, Casserly announced his continued vitality through the care he took with his personal appearance. He had a full head of white hair and a mustache. Both were neatly trimmed. He always wore a freshly pressed suit and a vest, and every crease was knife-sharp.

Casserly had sat through every word of the testimony. He was loaded for bear. He was not given to brief answers.

Q (by Rothenberg):And in your coverage of the Legislature and all these agencies, then you have situations where public officials, Legislators, Government officials themselves want to remain anonymous?

A (by Casserly): Absolutely. In fact, I brought with me something that I think might be helpful. It's a classic description, and it's very brief. If I may just quote from that—

Q: Please. ... Who wrote that?

> A: This was written by John R. Finnegan, Sr., and Patricia
> Hirl. It's a chapter called "Protecting Sources." Chapter V.
> MR. HANNAH: Objection on the ground of hearsay.

The objection was overruled.

> A: In the essence, it says that anonymous sources are a way of
> doing business and that the protection of these sources is impor-
> tant. It says the reasons for protecting confidential sources are
> very often the fact that many of these people are at risk. ...
> they're afraid of loss of jobs, they're afraid of loss of respect in
> the community if their names are used, they're afraid of public
> reprobation, public disdain if their names are used. ...
> Keeping your word is not something of concern only to
> journalists. All of us believe in it. It's an operating principle in
> which businesses conduct business. It's not the uniquely
> American view. It's a concept that a man's word or a woman's
> word is as good as his bond, and it's a matter of truth, it's a mat-
> ter of reliability, of people's trustworthiness in dealing with each
> other. After all, a promise is a promise, and it has—it is not
> exclusively done in journalism. It's a way of life. ... This is a case
> where honor was violated, where trust was ignored, and where
> questions will forever be raised about the danger of giving
> information to newspapers. And in effect, the impact here ... is
> that future trust is endangered. There will be feelings that in the
> future, who can trust newspapers to give them information?

The jurors may have tuned out a bit during some of the testimony, but not this testimony. He was our best witness. There
were no questions.

It was noon on Thursday, July 14. The trial had gone on eight
days.

Rothenberg rested. We had presented our case.

CHAPTER TWENTY-THREE

Next: Their Best Witness

Fitzmaurice called Tim McGuire, the managing editor of the *Star Tribune*, as his lead witness. It was not an idle choice. Lead witnesses are like first impressions. They present a powerful and lasting image in the jury's mind of the strength of your case. They establish the foundation and lay out the principal arguments. Everything that follows flows from their testimony.

McGuire had worked for papers in Michigan, Texas, Florida, and now, Minneapolis. He had been hired in 1979, replacing Nimmer as managing editor of the afternoon *Star*.

The *Star* folded in early 1982, and was merged into the morning *Tribune*. There had been a genuine rivalry between the two papers, and there were few survivors from the *Star*. McGuire was one of them, though his initial title at the combined *Star Tribune* was the lesser one of managing editor for features, his slot in October 1982. By the time of the trial, he had climbed back to his old position of managing editor, period.

McGuire was a classic grind. After he came to Minneapolis, he enrolled in night law school and, after five years, got his degree cum laude in 1987. He combined admirable work habits with the personality of a teacher's pet. His superiors adored him. Not all of his subordinates shared that view.

As a general rule, journalists do not make good witnesses. They are a lot like cops: they are cynical, they like having power over lesser mortals, and they have a lot of trouble relating to civilians, particularly when they are getting second-guessed in a courtroom. Lou Gelfand had been a disaster for the defense. Mike Finney had overplayed his part. Frank Wright and Joel Kramer had been acceptable, but hardly warm and sympathetic. If anyone knew how to gain the sympathy of a jury, it would be Fitzmaurice's so-called client, Tim McGuire. The week that McGuire had spent at the defendant's table, furiously scribbling notes, would pay off. He had gotten a feel for the courtroom and the trial, and he had learned what to say and what not to say when it came time for him to testify.

Fitzmaurice had McGuire discuss the meeting of editors on October 27 and the various options available to the paper other than breaking its promise, all of which were, of course, unacceptable to them.

Fitzmaurice then questioned McGuire about the original article that had appeared in the *Star Tribune* on October 28.

> Q (by Fitzmaurice): Now in your judgment, was the underlying event "newsworthy"?
>
> A (by McGuire): Yes, as I think is evidenced by the fact that we ended up with what we call a double-barreled lead in the story.
>
> Q: What does that mean?
>
> A: That means that we got two—that means that we got two facts in the same lead. That we said that "Court records show that DFL lieutenant governor candidate Marlene Johnson was convicted more than 12 years ago on a misdemeanor charge." … But the second barrel of the lead was that "It was given to reporters Wednesday by Dan Cohen, a friend and political associate of Independent Republican candidate Wheelock Whitney."
>
> Q: Mr. McGuire, in 1982 what was your view of under what circumstances it was appropriate not to honor an agreement of confidentiality?
>
> A: To be honest, prior to October 27, 1982, I had never really considered it. My view that day was that when the knowledge of who the source was has a substantial effect on the newsworthiness of the story and the readers' understanding or mis-

understanding of the real story, then that source ought to be named, and without question, that's a very rare thing. But there are cases in which the newsworthiness of who that source is is at least as important as the basic information conveyed in the story, and I felt this was one of those cases.

Q: And why was it that in your view the newsworthiness of the source was important as the underlying information?

A: In this case, an emissary of the Whitney campaign had leaked information that had been buried deep in the files when it was many points behind in the polls, and—just before the election, and the fact that in Minnesota that kind of campaign maneuver was being made seemed extremely important to me and seemed extreme—at least as important as a 12-year-old shoplifting record which had been vacated.

Fitzmaurice turned to the cases Rothenberg had used to impeach Gelfand and Kramer. McGuire had heard their testimony firsthand from the defendant's table. He knew the cases. He knew how to improve on Gelfand's botch job.

Q: Would you explain to the members of the jury why such stories appear in the *Star & Tribune*?

A: Well, Miss Minnesota, the first Miss Minnesota story, I believe her name was Ms. Bolich, was a particularly heartrending story in that she was going to the Miss America pageant, and she was claiming that what she had stolen were swimsuits and the like that she needed for that contest. So it was a very dramatic, upsetting, if you will, human interest story, and her arrest for that shoplifting was a very interesting human interest story.

Q: Now what do you mean by "context" in a journalistic sense?

A: The fact—say the second Miss Minnesota's name is Jane Smith. Jane Smith's five-year-old shoplifting conviction has absolutely no interest to us. There's thousands of people out in the world who have five-year-old shoplifting convictions, and we don't go around finding those out. However, if Jane Smith is a part of a group, say members of a certain law firm, and 12 of them have that kind of thing in their record, then it may have some context, especially if those 12 members of that law firm have recently committed a crime or are being suspected or investigated for something.

At that point, it has context and it has real meaning to the situation. The fact that it's on her record has no particular meaning.

McGuire then explained away the other stories Rothenberg had used to challenge Gelfand and Gelfand had booted: Biden, Ginsberg, Myerson, Isaacs.

> Q: Now there's been testimony in this trial, Mr. McGuire, with reference to the responsibility of journalists to keep their promises, and to protect their sources, to back their reporters. Now, what is your view, sir, on that subject? That is, that the responsibility of editors, reporters, and the newspaper in general to keep its promise to protect its sources, to back its reporters if they make a commitment?

> A: I feel strongly about all of those things. Promises are very important to me personally and professionally. I spend much of my time backing reporters, dealing with reporters who have had difficulties, trying to help them deal with difficult situations. Our reporters are crucial to anything that we do at the newspaper, they're the people at the front lines, and they're extremely important to us, and I want to back them wherever possible.

> Q: How about protecting their sources?

> A: Protection of sources is extremely important. I have more than once shown a willingness to go to jail to protect sources during my career. I have been asked if I was prepared to take that step, and I've said, yes, I am.

> Q: How do you reconcile that statement which you've just made which happened in this case in terms of not backing Lori Sturdevant's commitment, by overruling that decision and disclosing Mr. Cohen as the source?

> A: Because, as I said earlier, there are no absolutes in this business or any other. The world is full of grays, and the most important thing as a journalist is leveling with readers and making sure that to the best of my God-given ability we make that newspaper an honest, truthful, accurate reflection of what's going on,

and I don't want to leave readers confused about issues whenever I can avoid it.

It was a bravura performance. The jury did everything but applaud. I could see why McGuire had climbed so far so fast at the *Star Tribune*. The newspaper's other witnesses had stonewalled or moralized. There were no shades of gray. It was all black and white. They were right. I was wrong. They were absolutists, just as I had been, rigid and unyielding on every point.

McGuire had not really reached any different conclusions than his compatriots had. But his pretty packaging had disguised the same shopworn arguments they had used. McGuire could make you believe he was being reasonable, giving ground, conceding your arguments, when he really wasn't.

He was like a great halfback, who could, with a head fake, make you believe he was going to go off in one direction when he was heading exactly the opposite way. While you were still getting your feet untangled, he was crossing the goal line.

Marlene Johnson's shoplifting conviction was "newsworthy," so they published it, but then, though promises are "important," we also have to consider the gobbledygook about "context" and "double-barreled" leads, so they published my name, too. All of this in light of McGuire's lofty vision of "God-given" and "honest, truthful, accurate" journalism.

It was all smoke and mirrors. Years would pass before I would hear anyone do it so skillfully again.

"I feel your pain."

"Mistakes were made."

"We needed to do it to keep America heading in the right direction."

It would a take a masterful performance like a Bill Clinton press conference to match the direct testimony of Tim McGuire.

I looked over at the defense table as Fitzmaurice sat down. Counsel didn't give each other high-fives in Judge Knoll's courtroom, but if they did, Hannah would have given one to Fitzmaurice.

The defense was back in control of the case.

CHAPTER TWENTY-FOUR

Elliot Unchained

During the presentation of our case, the defense strategy had been to give jurors two options. One, I was a dirty trick artist who deserved to be burned for exposing Marlene Johnson. Two, my deal was no deal, because neither paper had it exclusively. They were hard theories to prove in the face of so much evidence that they had protected sources under similar circumstances, and exclusivity simply was not part of our deal.

So what was left for the defense to do?

Wait until it was their turn, and then give the jury a third option: the wise, compassionate, Minnesota-nice explanation of why it all had to happen the way they said it had to happen.

McGuire's role was to give the jury an expert's view on journalistic practices and ethics, and why newsworthiness, context, and the Minnesota ethos—an even more amorphous concept than Gelfand's "unspoken standards"—dictated that they disclose my identity. It was a less hard-edged version of the dirty tricks argument, the way painless lethal injection has replaced messy forms of capital punishment like hanging.

But no matter how much they prettied it up, the result was the same. Dead is dead. A promise is a promise. A lie is a lie.

> Q (by Rothenberg): I believe you said, Mr. McGuire, that you used words like "leveling with the reader," you had to "level with the reader," and that's why you had to identify Mr. Cohen, something like that? Did I state that correctly?
>
> A (by McGuire): Yeah, I think that's what I said.

Q: Okay. Well, Mr. McGuire, what we have here is not only a double-barreled story, but indeed there should be a triple-barreled story. Indeed, the triple barrel is probably more important than the other two, and that is the existence of a promise made by your reporter, Lori Sturdevant, to Dan Cohen, the overruling and dishonoring of that promise by the Editors, and the promise which is used to obtain that information in the first place.

And I notice in that very long article [that appeared on October 28] ... there is no mention of that fact, is there, Mr. McGuire?

A: No, there's not.

Q: All right. And what you are saying is that this is the first time you had ever encountered a situation like this where you had dishonored the promise of a reporter, or you, the editors of the newspaper, had dishonored the promise of the reporter?

A: Yes, it was my first time, that's right.

Q: All right. So you really weren't leveling with the readers on that issue, were you, Mr. McGuire?

A: Not on that disclosure, and I regret that.

Q: Now let's go to this issue of late revelations in political campaigns. It is true, is it not, that ... there have been several such articles in recent years while you have served as Managing Editor, is that not correct?

A: Not in campaigns of this magnitude, but perhaps there have been.

Q: You're aware, you recall, that in 1984 Robert Mattson was running against Joan Growe for the Democratic nomination for U.S. Senate to oppose Rudy Boschwitz. ... And this was on September 2nd, 1984, and the primary was to be held nine days later, Tuesday, September 11th, 1984. ... This article [in the September 2nd *Star Tribune*, entitled "Florida Deals Put Mattson Deep in Debt," written by Lori Sturdevant] goes into great detail about various financial problems of Robert Mattson in Florida going back to 1979, no reference to any criminal convictions, mind you, but just financial problems ... and then you see at the very end of that article that Mattson sent a telegram to the *Star & Tribune* claiming that the *Star & Tribune* is smearing him because they're bringing up all these things late in the campaign designed to destroy him as a candidate. Then you also have a response from Joel Kramer, who says,

We publish the story now because we only recently became aware of information which indicated to us that Mr. Mattson's financial situation and legal problems were significantly greater than we had realized. We have applied the same standards to this story that we apply to every story, and our only motive is to supply valuable information to our readers.

Did I read it accurately?

A: Yes, you read it accurately.

Q: Now, Mr. McGuire, what we have here is an example, is it not, of late campaign revelations in a political campaign. Are you also aware, Mr. McGuire, that Ms. Sturdevant testified that there were one or more confidential sources involved in this story?

A: No, I was not aware of that.

Q: Well, would you accept that?

A: (Witness nodded head up and down.)

Q: So what we have here, Mr. McGuire, do we not, is an example of revelations late in a campaign, by the *Star & Tribune* involving one or more confidential sources where the candidate involved, Robert Mattson, claims there is a smear, and where your editor, Joel Kramer, denies that in saying that the only motive is to supply valuable information to the reader.

So here your editor, when the *Star Tribune* does it, is saying that providing these revelations late in a campaign about a candidate is providing valuable information to readers?

A: Yes, that was current information about what Mr. Mattson was doing at that current time. He was in deep financial and legal trouble as he ran for the election.

Q: Mr. McGuire, could I point out again that this paragraph, we can go through the whole article, but it says,

The court records cover Mattson's three-year sojourn in Florida where he went in 1979 after losing the election of State Auditor. He returned to Minnesota in June '82.

So this covered the period of 1979 to 1982, didn't it, according to what the article says?

A: Well, I think you probably should continue reading the next paragraph which refers to his current problems.

Q: Okay. Talk of problems of the past year. We could read the whole article, because here you saw that we have problems of Trago, Incorporated, a firm jointly owned by Mattson and Michael Gibbs [who] failed to file income tax returns for 1981, 1982, and 1984.

A: Very recent activities for an '84 election.

Q: Okay. So here is an example of revelation late in a campaign, very late in a campaign involving troubles going back over a period of several years where your newspaper confronts an accusation and your editor says that that is valuable information for the readers?

A: Yeah, in this case.

Q: In that case.

A: In that particular case, that's right.

Q: We're talking about particular cases here. Let's take some more particular cases too, Mr. McGuire ... Recently, the *Star & Tribune* carried an article May 14th, 1988, only three days before a local School Board election in Rosemount/Apple Valley, entitled "Candidate Was Accused of Sex Harassment," and that article referred to, among other things, a charge made in 1983 ... and later on in the article it points out that apparently these discrimination complaints were dropped.

A: I don't recall the particular article, but I believe what you're reading.

Q: And so there your newspaper is providing information which is valuable to the readers even though [it] appear[s] only three days before an election?

A: I can't speak to that. I simply do not recall it to be able to explain the circumstances.

THE COURT: Just let him look at it and ask him if his recollection is refreshed.

Q: Well, then, it is true, is it not, as we discussed this article, "Candidate Was Accused of Sex Harassment," appeared three days before a local School Board election?

A: Yes, it did, in the context of what appears to be an active legal suit.

Q: All right. Mr. McGuire, just to try to conclude this particular article, ... the subject of the headline is a 1983 charge of sexual harassment which subsequently was dropped?

A: That's correct.

... Q: Okay. All right. And we've already had examples of things running three days before the election. So it's a fact, is it not, Mr. McGuire, that with full knowledge, Ms. Sturdevant had full knowledge that Mr. Cohen was a Whitney supporter, that Mr. Cohen was asking for a promise of confidentiality, that Ms. Sturdevant knew when the election was going to be held, that with full knowledge of all these things, Ms. Sturdevant made the promise of confidentiality, accepted the documents on the basis of that promise, and later, when the Editors decided to dishonor that promise, Ms. Sturdevant showed her anger by refusing to allow her name to be used on that article?

A: That's right, yes.

Q: And as a matter of fact, it's true, is it not, that besides the articles which we were speaking about, the articles on the Miss America USA candidates, the cartoon of the Miss America dressed as a jailbird, there have been scores, there have been hundreds of articles on shoplifting in the *Star & Tribune*; is that not correct?

A: When famous people are convicted or arrested for shoplifting, we publish it, yeah.

Q: And as a matter of fact, the *Star & Tribune* has run articles on policemen and ex-policemen, not at all famous, who have been arrested for shoplifting, have they not?

A: Oh, I think policemen are famous and there's a certain irony in policemen, former policemen being arrested for shoplifting.

Q: The same type of irony, sir, that would apply to a person who aspires to a position of being administrator of several billion dollars a year also being arrested for shoplifting?

A: Yes.

Q: And you are also aware of an article ... about a shoplifting or arrest of a former Miss America, Bess Myerson, in London, 18 years after that arrest took place?

A: I think the Bess Myerson case included a—she just paid the fine recently. But yes, shoplifting is an important issue.

Q: And it's also true that in the Bess Myerson case, is it not, that the original article from which that *Pioneer Press* article came was based on information from undisclosed sources.

A: I do not know that.

Q: If I showed you the original article in the *New York Daily News*, would that refresh your memory, sir?

A: I'm not doubting you, but I just do not know that.

Q: And in fact, in the … present situation, the two other news organizations involved, the Associated Press, [is] a very honorable news organization, would you not agree?

A: Yes, very honorable.

Q: And WCCO-TV, a highly respected and honorable news organization, would you not agree?

A: I agree.

Q: And that both these news organizations made the decision that regardless of any quote, "newsworthiness," unquote, of the connection of Mr. Cohen to this information, that they decided that they were going to honor the promises of their reporters to Mr. Cohen, correct?

A: They did.

Q: And one would assume also that Ms. Sturdevant, [is] a highly experienced, capable reporter; am I not correct? The reporter that the editors decided should be the chief reporter in the governorship race, correct?

A: That's right.

Q: And that Ms. Sturdevant, a reporter with her experience and her ability, also determined that despite the quote, … "newsworthiness," unquote, of Mr. Cohen's giving her that information, that she was going to honor that promise to Mr. Cohen, correct?

A: Correct.

There were no beams of approval from the defendant's table when McGuire stepped down from the witness stand this time.

They had underestimated Rothenberg. So had the judge. So had I. In the beginning, Rothenberg had seemed to be in over his head. Not seemed to be. He *was* over his head.

But every day, he had gotten better. The judge had stopped correcting Rothenberg's mistakes. There were fewer objections from defendants and fewer rulings from the bench in their favor. Rothenberg had learned how to introduce evidence, how to frame questions, how to build a case. Rothenberg was a quick study. Bill Gates has described the type: you can teach anything to a guy with brains.

The raw recruit had become a cagey veteran. A week earlier, McGuire would have eaten him alive. By the time Rothenberg cross-examined him, he had become more than a match for the defendants—and for their lead witness. Rothenberg stripped away McGuire's glossy paint job, and underneath was the same tired old junker with the turned-back odometer the defendants had tried to sell before.

Why was my involvement in the incident newsworthy, but the promise made to me, the breaking of the promise, and the reporter's demand for anonymity not newsworthy? Why was it acceptable to publish damaging material about a candidate nine days before an election, or even three days before an election, but not six days?

Why was a twelve-year-old shoplifting conviction less newsworthy than a year-old shoplifting conviction? Under cross-examination, McGuire's explanations gave way to the same kind of hairsplitting attempts to distinguish the undistinguishable that had characterized all his predecessors on the witness stand.

McGuire had been a great witness on direct. On cross-examination, he had faithfully followed what undoubtedly were his instructions from Fitzmaurice: give short answers, do not fence with opposing counsel, maintain a respectful, impersonal demeanor. But facts are stubborn things.

Our case was simple. They had made a promise and broken it.

They had made their case much more complicated. By thrashing around for a theory that would work—dirty tricks, exclusivity, context, newsworthiness—they had lost focus. Every time they tried a new approach, the more skillfully Rothenberg skewered them with the inconsistencies in their own behavior.

CHAPTER TWENTY-FIVE

The Inexpert Witness

David Lawrence, the next witness, was an uptown version of Tim McGuire—but he was no McGuire. He was publisher and chairman of the *Detroit Free Press*. He had been called as an expert witness on journalistic practices and ethics. McGuire was a blue-collar guy who had fought hard to overcome his physical disabilities to get ahead. He was the kind of witness our jury would tend to have some compassion for. Bernie Casserly, our expert, had been the same sort, determined to keep on going until they found him slumped over his old Underwood. Believe their testimony or not, McGuire and Casserly were colorful, sympathetic characters.

Lawrence was not cut from the same cloth. He was a stuffed shirt. His fulminating about the evils lurking behind the motives of confidential sources was old stuff. Fitzmaurice posed a long hypothetical based on his version of the Johnson incident and asked him how he would have handled it. Lawrence gave a windy and predictable response that the "stories that ran were reasonable and with honor."

Finally, the judge had had enough.

The following discussion took place out of the hearing of the jury:

> THE COURT: I'm sorry to interrupt, but what is the relevance of this testimony to a contract action or a fraud action? ... What does this guy have to do with it? ... We've been going around and around with this. I don't know who started it. I don't know who brought this issue in the case. I can't even

remember where it started, but it seems that we're getting a seminar on this, paper practices, and I don't know what it has to do with contracts or misrepresentation. Anyway, can you ask a few more questions and—he's giving a dissertation here.

MR. FITZMAURICE: I'll cut it short.

He didn't, of course, and the two of them rambled on, trying to explain why honor and credibility justified lying to a source. Only this time, the judge's eye-rolling was directed at the defendants and not at us. Rothenberg began his cross-examination:

Q (by Rothenberg): But the salient point is this, is it not, Mr. Lawrence, that you're not appearing as a disinterested expert witness on the facts and principles of this case, but basically you're appearing on behalf of your employer, which is also the employer of the *St. Paul Pioneer Press Dispatch*?

A (by Lawrence): You're exactly wrong. The most important thing I own is my integrity, and it's not for sale to anyone, including the company I work for.

Q: But the fact is the company you work for and the company the *Pioneer Press Dispatch* is owned by is the same company, correct?

A: Yes, sir.

Q: Now, Mr. Lawrence, you said you have seen the article in the *Star & Tribune* on this case?

A: (Witness nodded head up and down.)

Q: And it's—the original article identified Mr. Cohen?

A: Yes, sir.

Q: It's right up there on the board. And that's a very long article, isn't it?

A: I don't know if it's yes, no. What makes a very long article? I'm not being contentious—

THE COURT: Just hold it, now. Just a second. If you don't have an answer, say you don't understand the question, but I don't want a speech from every question. And I'd like to have your questions not repetitive.

MR. ROTHENBERG: All right.

THE COURT: Ask him a question.

MR. ROTHENBERG: Okay.

Q: Could you tell us, perhaps how many column inches that article is?

A: The honest answer is I don't know, sir.

THE COURT: That's a good answer.

Q: But surely there is a general principle or general consensus within the journalistic profession, as there is among human society in general, is there, about the necessity, the moral and ethical and practical necessity of keeping one's word?

A: I certainly think that one of the guiding principles of a good society is integrity, yes, sir.

Q: And that guiding principle is the principle which was not followed by the newspapers in this case; is that not correct?

A: That particular guiding principle, yes, sir.

MR. ROTHENBERG: Thank you, sir.

MR. FITZMAURICE: Nothing further, Your Honor.

THE COURT: You may step down, Mr. Lawrence.

Why David Lawrence? They could have gotten damn near anyone as an expert—why not someone who wasn't one of their own employees? Despite our own meager resources, and given the reluctance to testify against these defendants among those I contacted before Casserly, we still found an expert with no personal or professional ties to us. So why did the defendants call David Lawrence?

The answer is, because David Lawrence was the embodiment of what newspapers are all about.

Lawrence got up on the witness stand and did what newspaper pashas do when they are running their newspapers. He preached. He judged. He patronized. He refused to concede even the most minor point: the article was long. The habits of a lifetime, performed daily to a captive audience of underlings and distant readers.

But not this time. Instead of the usual respectful reception, he was challenged and interrupted.

Calling his own integrity into question? He bridled at the suggestion, though he had no reluctance to sit in judgment on the integrity of others.

Running on a bit with his words of wisdom though the judge has expressed his impatience? Whatever else you do in a court-room, you don't annoy a judge. The jury takes its cues from the judge. Rothenberg would always apologize when he messed up.

David Lawrence couldn't quite bring himself to shorten his answers or say he was sorry. He was not used to being criticized or told what to do, and he made it obvious he didn't like it. Lawrence exemplified the misconception these defendants had of how the world worked, because they had never had to function in it the same way everyone else did.

Fitzmaurice should have known better. If McGuire couldn't do it, nobody could.

Maybe that was their problem. Nobody could.

If the defendants' witnesses kept asserting their moral recti-tude, ignoring the evidence we kept throwing in their faces, and if we kept asking them whether breaking their word was part of that moral code, they were going to continue to appear foolish and hypocritical.

CHAPTER TWENTY-SIX

The Angry Man

After Lawrence's testimony finally reached its long-awaited conclusion, David Hall took the stand. Hall was executive editor of the *Pioneer Press* in October 1982 and the first person who made the decision to break the promise of anonymity to me. Hall was a feisty Southerner who had started as a reporter and worked at newspapers in Tennessee, Chicago, and Denver. He left St. Paul in 1984 and was editor of a paper called the *Bergen County Record* in New Jersey at the time of the trial.

In the news hierarchy at the *Pioneer Press*, the reporter, Bill Salisbury, reported to Doug Hennes, the city editor, who reported to Deborah Howell, the managing editor, who reported to David Hall, who reported to John Finnegan, the editor in chief.

Hall made his decision to name me immediately after he learned from Hennes about Salisbury's deal with me. Hall was furious. Salisbury not only had failed to get a routine promise of exclusivity from me, he hadn't bothered to check first with Hennes, even though the reporters' manual stated clearly that was something he should have done.

The *Pioneer Press's* normal decision-making process was just as cumbersome as the *Star Tribune's*. But if there were any bureaucratic constraints on Hall, he ignored them. His instant call to name me was characteristic of his hair-trigger temper. He may have been motivated as much by wanting to punish Salisbury as to expose my role. Now, six years later, Hall was being second-guessed and once again, his irascibility was getting the best of him.

Hall was Hannah's lead witness.

> Q (by Hannah): All right. Now, were you aware that Mr. Salisbury disagreed with the decision that you made?
>
> A (by Hall): Yeah, I was.
>
> Q: Did that enter into your judgment at all to name Mr. Cohen in the article?
>
> A: Not really.

The cross-examination by Rothenberg followed.

> Q (by Rothenberg): Mr. Hall, your article does not reflect the fact, does it, that Mr. Cohen not only requested confidentiality, but actually was promised confidentiality by your reporter, Mr. Salisbury, and indeed did not provide that material to your reporter, Mr. Salisbury, until he received that promise of confidentiality? That is not reflected in your article?
>
> A (by Hall): That is not reflected in the article. You are right.
>
> Q: All right. And we're going to be talking about your obligation to your readers for completeness and accuracy under that criterion which you have mentioned. Should that fact not have been mentioned in the article?
>
> A: I don't think it should have been in that article, no.
>
> Q: You don't think it should have been?
>
> A: No.
>
> Q: So the readers, by your opinion, don't have to know that the newspaper broke its promise to Mr. Cohen, that's something the public doesn't have to know?
>
> A: I don't think that it was particularly relevant in this article.
>
> Q: I see. So … you felt that the public, although it had the right to know Mr. Cohen's name, in violation of the promise made to him by Mr. Salisbury, did not have the right to know that a promise to Mr. Cohen was made and broken?
>
> A: The article, the decision to use Mr. Cohen's name in this was—one of the—excuse me. If I might, I need to explain this. … I don't think [t]hat I felt that they didn't have the right. I didn't think it was necessary in this article.

Q: So the—your criterion of completeness in allowing the public the right to know does have limits when the paper might be embarrassed?

MR. HANNAH: Objection, argumentative.

THE COURT: Sustained.

Q: As a matter of fact, right around the same time that your story appeared identifying Mr. Cohen, there was another story in the sports section about various North Star [hockey] players attacking on an anonymous basis the then coach of the team [Glen Sonmor], and they were all allowed to remain anonymous, were they not?

A: I don't recall?

Q: It contains such statements as

"He may have been a good coach at one [time], but he doesn't handle the team well behind the bench," one player said [last] week.

Another said, "The real reason we lost in Montreal was lack of control behind the bench.."

A third said, "We never practice the right things."

A fourth came up with a severe indictment. "I'm fed up to the top of my head with Glen playing favorites."

So far, none of Sonmor's critics would stick his neck on the block and openly challenge the North Stars coach.

So the question is this, sir, that the *Pioneer Press* on occasion, and indeed, right around the time that it was identifying Mr. Cohen, ran a similar story—well, another story with unidentified sources, where the public, on the basis of your argument, might have had a good reason to know who these players were who were anonymously attacking the coach?

A: I think they would have been interested in knowing.

Q: Uh-huh. But in this case where the public would have been interested in knowing the names of these players, you honored the promises of confidentiality made to these players?

A: I don't know that Charlie [Hallman, the sportswriter] promised them confidentiality, but he perhaps he did.

Q: To repeat again, the story says, "So far, none of Sonmor's critics will stick his neck on the block and openly challenge the North Stars coach."

A: I read the paragraph. I don't know what Mr. Hallman talked to these players about when he gathered that story. I assume he told them that he wouldn't use their names.

Q: And in this case with the hockey players and Mr. Hallman, you did honor the promises of confidentiality?

A: I suppose we did.

Q: Okay. Let me examine this [reporters' manual] with you, and where it says, … "a reporter should check with his superior before promising anonymity or confidentiality." That indicates that the reporter can indeed make a promise of anonymity or confidentiality, correct?

A: It could be interpreted that way.

Q: Uh-huh. And it does not provide for any sanctions against a reporter?

A: It does not?

Q: It does not?

A: No, it does not.

Q: Okay. And indeed, the language here is considerably less strong than in others. I notice you have a section on courtesy titles, and it's capitalized, "We DO NOT," and "DO NOT" is capitalized, "use Ms. in any circumstances." Do you see that here?

A: I see it.

Q: And you don't say anywhere here "We do not—" "Reporters should not," or "Reporters do not promise anonymity before getting approval of the editors." It simply does not say that here, does it, sir?

A: It says what it says.

Q: It says what it says. All right. Okay. Thank you. … And I notice another section of this employee handbook, your Exhibit Number 28, regarding some very stern admonitions on library files.

Clippings and photographs must be signed out when such material is removed from the library. Failure to do so could result in disciplinary action. Anyone taking clippings and/or photos from our library for personal use or use in other publications without permission of the department head could be dismissed.

In other words, the language you apply for the offense of taking out library files without permission is considerably stronger than the language used on confidential sources, is it not, for reporters?

A: That's your interpretation of it.

Q: Well, I think as you point out, the material reads for itself. And as a matter of fact, Mr. Salisbury was not disciplined for making his promise of confidentiality, was he?

A: No, he was not.

Q: Okay. So the only person punished as a result of the dishonoring of that promise was the source, Mr. Cohen himself; that's correct, isn't it?

A: That he was punished?

Q: (Mr. Rothenberg nodded head up and down.)

A: That's your judgment, sir, not mine, that he was punished.

Q: Well, so you wouldn't consider firing from a job punishment?

A: As I said, that's your characterization. We reported a news story and people make up their minds of what they should do with that information.

Q: Okay. Now, Mr. Hall, we've talked about principles and obligations of the newspaper to its readers and to the general public, but you believe, do you not, that keeping your word, keeping the word of the newspaper to individuals and to the general public ... also ought to be an important policy of the newspaper?

A: It is a factor to be considered.

Q: A factor to be considered?

A: That's right.

Q: One hopes that it should be an important factor to be considered?

A: It is an important factor to be considered, but one of many.

Q: So keeping your promise, keeping your word, is ... only one issue to be considered among many?

A: Only one of many.

Q: One of many. Okay. Thanks.

By the time Hall left the witness stand, Rothenberg had gotten to the point where he was simply repeating Hall's answers to emphasize how resentful and unresponsive they sounded.

Though no one came out and said so, David Hall's disposition was a major reason all of us were in that courtroom. The *Star Tribune* stalled on its decision to use my name until its editors found out that the *Pioneer Press* was going to do it. If Hall hadn't decided as he had, it's unlikely the *Star Tribune*, despite all their rationalizations, would have wanted to be out there breaking promises all by themselves while three other media outlets kept theirs.

Hall provided them with the cover to break their promise and lambaste me.

Hannah's lead witness was no McGuire. If Hall didn't have such a quick trigger, he would have made a better witness.

But Hall was Hall, and Cohen was Cohen, and that's why we were where we were.

CHAPTER TWENTY-SEVEN

It Isn't Over 'til It's Over

Exclusivity. Dirty tricks. Minnesota nice. Three down, or least crippled. Time to trot out a new theory.

Fitzmaurice recalled Frank Wright.

Once more, Fitzmaurice went through the decision-making process at the *Star Tribune* the night of October 27. But this time, Wright gave the papers' motives a new spin.

> Q (by Fitzmaurice): All right. Would you elaborate on that, sir?
>
> A (by Wright): The issues, as we saw them at the time, were much as they have been discussed here by others. Basically I saw it as a conflict between two general and widely held values in the newspaper business. One is the question of who can grant confidentiality and what are you[r] responsibilities as an editor in upholding that grant of confidentiality. The other issue ... was what do you need to do to best serve the greatest number of readers, at, in this case, a time when a highly contested election campaign was coming to a close and is almost over.
>
> Those were the two main issues, ... confidentiality on the one hand and serving readers on the other hand.

The hardball witnesses, Lou Gelfand and David Hall, had been failures. The over-the-top moralizer, Tim McGuire, had his moments, but under Elliot's cross-examination had been unconvincing. David Lawrence was a disaster.

Fitzmaurice tried to split the difference with Wright. Temperamentally, Wright was cool and detached. He appeared less rigid and confrontational than either Gelfand or Hall, yet he could hew to the party line just as closely as they had.

He had avoided the ethical flights of fancy that had tripped up McGuire and Lawrence, but he could make pretty much the same points by posing the papers' motives in terms of professional journalistic standards. He had posed a conundrum hypothesis: how do we serve the greatest number of people? By telling the truth to one and lying to the multitudes, or lying to one and telling the truth to the multitudes? Obviously, the papers' first duty was to their readers. Like our Gelfand fork, this was another one of those false choices lawyers lovingly construct as traps for the unwary.

By this time, though, the defense had tried so many theories to explain why they had broken their promise, one more or less didn't matter. We could all sense the mood in the courtroom had become "Let's get this thing over with."

Still, there was more. Dave Floren had been my supervisor at Martin/Williams at the time I was fired. Floren was a quick study and an adept office politician, the Martin/Williams version of Tim McGuire. He was the trim, handsome picture of the dashing advertising executive as he brushed past our table and strode confidently onto the witness stand.

Fitzmaurice wanted him to establish three major points for the defense:

First, Fitzmaurice gave dirty tricks still another airing. Since Floren was not an employee of either the *Star Tribune* or the *Pioneer Press*, we couldn't dredge up newspaper articles to impeach him. He testified that "my own characterization of something like that would be that it was a campaign dirty trick."

Second, Floren testified that I had received and retained funds from the Whitney campaign. The words he used were "He benefited from it directly."

Third, Floren tried to establish that I had resigned and was not fired. He testified that during my conversation with Haag, I had said, "Well, if you feel that way about it, I have no choice but to resign." There was also a little fact problem to explain. Why was it that, after I told him about my meetings with the press on the afternoon of October 27, the day *before* the articles appeared, he had not reacted to, much less criticized me for, my actions?

Fitzmaurice knew Rothenberg would raise that issue on cross-examination, so he tried to pre-empt it. Floren testified on direct, "I was in a hurry, and I was also on my way out, so [it was] probably [a] very subdued reaction. But I guess my thought was at the time I was rather stunned on hearing this. And as usual in a case like this, when I received information like that, I wanted more time to think about it, what really the impact of that was."

On cross-examination, Rothenberg produced financial records that showed despite the dirty tricks, Martin/Williams had received $3,438 from the Whitney campaign for my work, including the $500 check made out to me from the Fallon agency, which I had endorsed over to Martin/Williams. Rothenberg also produced a Martin/Williams memo to me from the Profit Sharing Committee containing the phrase "you were terminated."

So much for my having profited personally or resigned my position. There were no further questions from defense counsel.

When Floren left the witness stand, he did not cross by our table again. He stayed on the defense side of the courtroom. His step was not quite so jaunty.

Hannah next called Deborah Howell, who had been managing editor of the *Pioneer Press* in October 1982, and, by the time of the trial, had become editor of both the *St. Paul Pioneer Press* and the *St. Paul Dispatch*. She had been a reporter and editor at the *Star* before moving to the St. Paul papers. Howell had achieved the highest position of any woman in the journalism game in the Twin Cities. She deserved it. She was likeable, earthy, and had the additional virtue of not taking herself terribly seriously. By conventional standards, she was not a great beauty, but she dressed superbly and radiated wit and personality.

I did not like seeing her on the witness stand testifying for the defense. Hannah began his direct examination:

> Q (by Hannah): All right. Now, Ms. Howell, could you tell me when you first became aware of the circumstances that are involved in the lawsuit?
>
> A (by Howell): I walked into the newsroom late in the afternoon and I noticed Doug Hennes in conversation with Bill Salisbury, and it was obvious to me something was up. So I walked over and said, "What is going on?" And Doug says, "You don't want to know." ... I said, "Oh, yes, I do," and he said, "Oh, no, you don't," and I subsequently found out about the issue with the shoplifting conviction of Marlene Johnson, and I agreed that I did not want to be involved in it.
>
> Q: And why is that, Ms. Howell?
>
> A: Marlene's a personal friend of mine.

When I looked at the jury, the women were hanging on every word. Howell was the first witness that they really seemed to identify with. I cringed when she testified that Marlene—not "Marlene Johnson," but just "Marlene"—was a "personal friend." With that one remark, she brought Marlene into the courtroom as a woman like herself, a woman of style and class, not a befuddled shoplifter. I could almost hear the gears grinding in the jurors' minds. If this woman was Marlene's friend, then Marlene was someone like Howell, a person we like and respect. Therefore, Marlene should be vindicated, and we should find for the defendants. I couldn't wait until Hannah got through with her.

Fortunately, Hannah only asked a few more questions.

Unfortunately for Hannah, Rothenberg had an agenda.

He got Howell to admit that for many years the St. Paul papers had published lists of the names and addresses of people convicted of shoplifting in the local courts. He also produced an article that read,

> The *Dispatch* has obtained 49 pages of the controversial report
> [of a Minnesota Legislative Audit commission criticizing the
> actions of a previous governor, Wendell Anderson] from a state
> government source, who does not wish to be identified.

Howell admitted that this was another instance where her
paper had honored their promise to the source, though the article
ran only a week before Anderson was running for election for a
full term in the United States Senate. It was good stuff, but the jury
had tuned out our good stuff regarding Howell. She was a star.

"Elliot," I said during a break in the questioning, "she's killing
us. The jury loves her. Get her the hell out of there." And he did.

It was late afternoon, Friday, July 15, the ninth day of the trial.

> MR. FITZMAURICE: Did the Court plan to recess at 4:30?
> THE COURT: (Whereupon, the Court nodded his head up
> and down.)
> MR. FITZMAURICE: I can put Mr. Finney on. I don't
> know that we'll complete him. We have one short witness on
> Monday, who is Mr. Anderson, and then ... we'll rest.
> THE COURT: Well, if you put Finney on, you would want
> to cross-examine him again?
> MR. ROTHENBERG: Yeah.
> MR. FITZMAURICE: I would guess we rest within an hour
> on Monday.

The court recessed until Monday.

Finney again? I'd seen his game. Nothing to worry about
there. Anderson? Never heard of him.

I had a mindless weekend at the racetrack. Even won a few
bucks. It seemed like a good omen.

CHAPTER TWENTY-EIGHT

Perry Mason Lives!

On Monday morning when the trial resumed, the defense called David Anderson. Anderson had been a reporter at the *Star Tribune* for nine years and an assistant city editor for two and a half years. I had no idea what his involvement in the case had been. I figured they had probably called him as another so-called expert claiming it was okay to burn a source. Fitzmaurice began his direct examination:

> Q (by Fitzmaurice): Now you have, have you not, taken a special interest in the subject matter of investigative reporting?
>
> A (by Anderson): Yes, I have.
>
> Q: Would you tell the members of the jury what your experience has been in the field of investigative reporting and to what extent you have either lectured or published in the field?
>
> A: I've published a book, a textbook entitled *Investigative Reporting*, which, I believe was—it's gone through six printings and it's been used on more campuses than any of the other books on the topic.
>
> MR. ROTHENBERG: We want to raise an objection that this witness has not been previously identified as an expert witness on investigative reporting.
>
> MR. FITZMAURICE: I haven't offered him as such.
>
> MR. ROTHENBERG: Well, your reference is made, apparently, to a book, and … there's been no opportunity on the part of Counsel to read his book.
>
> THE COURT: Mr. Fitzmaurice is not going to elicit an opinion or expert testimony from the witness. I think he can proceed.

Q: All right. Now, let me address your attention to the time frame of October of 1982, and specifically October the 27th of 1982 which was one day prior to the publication in the *Star & Tribune* of an article which is the subject of the lawsuit. Are you with me?

Anderson testified that on the afternoon of October 27, he had been asked if he knew how to find expunged records. He said he thought he could, and he was given a photocopy of Johnson's conviction and sent to verify it. He went to the archives in St. Paul, located where her record was kept, and "then, in order to take that volume off the shelf and examine it, you have to sign it out, sign your name, the date and the time. ... And I did it, and examined it." It was identical to the photocopy he had brought with him. "And I got the guard's permission to photocopy it ... and asked the guard if I could use the telephone on his desk because the person who had signed it out a day or two before I did was a name I recognized. ... The last name signed before I signed mine was Gary Flakne, the former Hennepin County attorney, ... the day before I had it."

Q (by Fitzmaurice): Now, then, what did you do after you made the observation of Mr. Flakne's name on the sign-out sheet?
A (by Anderson): I called him.
Q: Were you able to reach him?
A: Yes.
Q: And did you have a conversation with Mr. Flakne?
A: Yes, I did.
Q: Would you relate that?
MR. ROTHENBERG: Your honor, I'm going to object if there's going to be any hearsay on the part of what Mr. Flakne said to Mr. Anderson. Mr. Anderson can testify what he said, but not what Mr. Flakne said to him.
THE COURT: Mr. Fitzmaurice?

MR. FITZMAURICE: We're offering it, Your Honor, pursuant to Rule 613 (b), which is offered as direct impeachment of the testimony of Mr. Flakne.

THE COURT: Have you disclosed—disclosed as to Mr. Flakne?

MR. FITZMAURICE: We examined Flakne on this and asked him whether or not it was a fact that he had a conversation—I think he said—

THE COURT: I recall the testimony of Flakne. I think the rule requires—at least the rule contemplates a practice of requiring prior disclosure to the witness, had an opportunity to explain before offering a prior inconsistent statement into evidence. In the appropriate case, the Court has discretion to waive this foundation—

MR. FITZMAURICE: Well, to the extent that we have confronted him with that in open court and indicated that, you know, obviously we have a basis for that, but no, I have never sat down Flakne, and said we were going to call Anderson to rebut it.

MR. ROTHENBERG: But ... the witness must be given a specific opportunity to explain or deny the same. ... This never happened with Flakne. ... That should have been brought forward in the examination or the cross-examination of Flakne.

THE COURT: All right. Here's what I'm going to do. I'm going to allow the testimony to go forward and ... you can bring him back here if you want to.

MR. ROTHENBERG: That's under the Federal Rule. But under the Minnesota Rule, the witness has to be given the prior opportunity.

THE COURT: Where's that?

MR. FITZMAURICE: Well, I maintain that we have given him the opportunity. Now, wait a minute, would you, Elliot. Don't interrupt me. The witness was in court and we confronted the witness in court and asked him whether or not it wasn't a fact that he was contacted by a reporter and that he told a reporter—

THE COURT: What's he going to say?

> MR. FITZMAURICE: This guy? He's going to say that what
> Flakne told him in the course of the conversation was that he
> was over there and, he admits, sent by Dan Cohen to check this
> information out. That's what he's going to say.

I was reeling. The entire defense up to this point had been just been a feint, a diversion to set me up and soften up the jury for their main attack.

They were going to claim that Flakne said he was merely doing my bidding and that I had been behind the plot to expose Johnson from the outset.

If it were true, then not only did they have a new theory for voiding their promise—they had found out about my role from an independent source—but I had lied to the jury all along when I said I had not heard about Johnson's conviction until I met with Flakne and Co., the morning *after* he obtained the records.

"We have one short witness on Monday," Fitzmaurice had said Friday afternoon.

One short witness and one big surprise.

> THE COURT: I think what I'm going to do is discharge the
> jury for a moment. I think this is kind of an important point.
> And you can put your arguments on the record.

The jury was sent out of the courtroom and the lawyers argued the point at the bench.

> THE COURT: Mr. Fitzmaurice, you have Mr. Anderson on
> the stand, and your intention, as I understand it, now, is to
> impeach by means of extrinsic evidence through Mr. Anderson
> Mr. Flakne's earlier testimony regarding what he said in regard
> to the archives? Is that a fair statement of your position?
> MR. FITZMAURICE: Yes. ... We are moving pursuant to
> Rule 613 (b) which is the prior statement of witnesses, and (b)
> provides that "extrinsic evidence of a prior inconsistent state-
> ment by a witness is not admissible unless the witness is afford-
> ed a prior opportunity to explain or deny the same, and the

opposite party is afforded the opportunity to interrogate him thereon for the interest of justice otherwise required."

THE COURT: Well, let me just make sure I understand it. As you're aware, this is a fairly rare[ly] used rule. As I understand the rule, it provides that a witness who's being impeached ha[s] a prior opportunity to explain or deny the same, and as I understand it, your [Fitzmaurice's] position is he was given that opportunity when he was testifying here earlier. I think Mr. Rothenberg's position ... is that he must be given the opportunity, and the rule specifically says "prior thereto"?

MR. ROTHENBERG: Yes, sir.

THE COURT: To explain or deny any inconsistency that may be shown in his prior testimony. ... All right. I'm going to require that Mr. Flakne be given a prior opportunity to come here and to respond to Mr. Rothenberg's explanation, and cross-examination then, by you, Mr. Fitzmaurice, before I will allow Mr. Anderson to provide the impeaching testimony.

Well, a tactical victory anyway. Anderson stepped off the witness stand—for the time being. Flakne would have the opportunity to deny what Anderson was about to say before he said it.

While I was trying to round up Flakne, I asked Gail if she would go over to the public library and try to find a copy of Anderson's textbook. We might be able to find something useful in it.

In the meantime, the show must go on. Rothenberg called our final witness, John Finnegan, who was editor of the *Pioneer Press* and of the *Dispatch* in October 1982 and David Hall's boss. For years, Finnegan had written a weekly column in the Sunday edition of the *Pioneer Press*. The column was a gold mine of fulminations against all who would reveal or compel a reporter to reveal a confidential source. Rothenberg began his cross-examination:

Q (by Rothenberg): Now, you do regard the protection of confidential sources as very important, don't you, sir?

A (by Finnegan): Yes, I do.

Q: Okay. And as a matter of fact, in one of your columns written a few months before the Cohen case, you referred to the violation of a confidential source as a, quote, "dirty trick," unquote; isn't that correct, sir?

A: I can't recall the precise column, but I may have.

Q: Okay, if I were to tell you that the column was entitled "Have You Met Megan Carter" and it was dated October 4th, 1981—

A: Yes, I remember the column.

Rothenberg went through several more columns Finnegan had written advocating shield laws to protect reporters from revealing their confidential sources. He then quoted from a Finnegan column that stated these laws "... are especially important in the field of investigative reporting where sources may fear for their lives, their jobs or the safety of their families if their identities are revealed, particularly in highly sensitive cases."

Q (by Rothenberg): Okay. And also you say, "It is clear that unless there is some protection of the right to gather news and protect sources, the quality and flow of news will be seriously impaired."

A (by Finnegan): That's correct.

MR. ROTHENBERG: Thank you.

THE COURT: Could we—Mr. Flakne is here, Mr. Rothenberg. Could we take his testimony?

We had saved Finnegan for last. We thought that letting the jury know that the editor of the St. Paul papers actually had used the magic words *dirty trick* to describe the act of one of his own revealing a confidential source would be a devastating blow to the defense.

But Finnegan was practically smirking when he left the witness stand. He had amiably conceded his multiple inconsistencies. Who cared? That dirty trick stuff was old and boring.

There was a new twist to the tale.

It now appeared the case would hinge on what the jury believed Gary Flakne had or had not told a reporter on the day of our meeting about my role in the Johnson incident.

Would he admit he had said I had asked him to get the documents? Would he deny it?

Whatever he testified, would the jury believe him?

I didn't have a clue. I told Rothenberg I wanted to go back on the witness stand. Rothenberg told me to be quiet.

> Q (by Fitzmaurice): Mr. Flakne—
> A (by Flakne): Yes, sir?
> Q: —we've interrupted the testimony of Mr. David Anderson who's a reporter with the *Tribune*, or was in 1982. I'll represent to you, sir, that Mr. Anderson's testimony is going to be to the effect that he placed a telephone call to you, I believe on October the 27th, 1982, and he was calling from the archives of the—where the court records were kept, and in the course of that conversation he asked you, in effect, why it was that you had signed out the Marlene Johnson record.
> First of all … do you deny a conversation with Mr. Anderson?
> A: I don't—excuse me, I don't recollect a specific conversation with a Mr. Anderson. I don't know Mr. Anderson.
> Q: The substance of Mr. Anderson's testimony is going to be, was that he asked you whether or not you were part of some effort to bring this information to the attention of the press and that your response was, in substance, that you had been asked to do this by Mr. Cohen and that you were doing it, in effect, as a favor to Mr. Cohen.
> Would you deny that, sir, or would you care, in any way, to explain it?
> A: I could not tell you that that conversation took place. I have no specific recollection, specifically, of that conversation, but if that is Mr. Anderson's testimony, it is incorrect insofar as I'm concerned. The reason I say that is because those were not true facts. Mr. Cohen did not send me over to the area where I picked up the records. Whether I was part of anything to bring

it to the press, I don't recall that question being asked. I doubt that that was asked.

MR. FITZMAURICE: Mr. Rothenberg?

Q (by Rothenberg): Just to confirm, Mr. Flakne, Mr. Cohen did not send you to get those materials, you did not do it on behalf of Mr. Cohen, is that correct?

A (by Flakne): Sir, I think I've already testified that that was— that that is not correct. Mr. Cohen did not send me over there.

When the campaign had found out about the documents, they had called Gary Flakne, because they didn't want to get their own hands dirty. He had been a good solider and had gone over and gotten them. He could have delivered them to the press then. But he didn't. He sensed the danger. He had done his bit, now it was someone else's turn.

So he had called a meeting and invited four other people, including me, hoping one would volunteer. I did.

The next thing Flakne knew, a reporter was on the phone asking him about his own involvement. Maybe, at that moment, Flakne had given me up. He had thought he had distanced himself, but here was Anderson, telling Flakne his fingerprints were all over the scene of the crime. He'd been found out because I'd bumbled around the capitol basement in my trench coat passing out envelopes with the adroitness of Inspector Clouseau.

"I did it for Dan Cohen," he might have said.

If that's the way it happened, I can understand it. I might have done the same thing.

Flakne didn't deny having had the conversation with Anderson. He didn't deny having *told* Anderson that he had done it for me. He testified that even though he had "no specific recollection" of the conversation with Anderson, the truth was that I had not asked to get the records, that he had *not* done it for me.

Fitzmaurice called Anderson back to the witness stand.

Q (by Fitzmaurice): Now, you said you placed the call to Mr. Flakne. Now, would you relate to the members of the jury your best recollection of the conversation?

A (by Anderson): I thought I would ask him why. ... I was expecting a fairly routine thing, answer, and I got what I considered a fairly routine answer, "Yes, I did it for Dan Cohen." He didn't say that he was sent over there. He didn't tell me he was sent over there, and if I told anybody that that's an error. I asked him how it came to be he ... went over there, and he said that Dan had asked him if he knew how to get those kinds of records, and he said he did, and that he volunteered to get them since he was going over to St. Paul that day anyhow.

Q: Then what did you do?

A: I wrote up somewhere between four and eight paragraphs as an insert for a story that I was told was being prepared by Lori Sturdevant, and sent it off to Lori's queue in the computer system, relaying what I just testified to.

Q: When you say relaying what you just testified to, what if anything did you say in your story relative to Mr. Cohen?

A: That Flakne said that he had obtained the records on behalf of Cohen and that it was part of the—their plan to distribute the information that she did have a criminal record, and I think [he] said that he had done it as a favor to Cohen because he was going over there.

Q: Did you see the story as it appeared the next day?

A: Yes, I did.

Q: And were your four to eight [paragraphs] in the story?

A: No, they weren't.

Q: Were any of them?

A: I only see one of them.

Q: Which one?

A: "A checkout log of court records in St. Paul Municipal Court archives indicates that the files on the Johnson case have been checked out only once in 1982 on Tuesday by Gary Flakne, former Hennepin County Attorney and a former I-R Legislator."

Q: Now, at the time you went over there and at the time you wrote the story, were you under any commitments, obligations, agreements, or anything of the kind pertaining to handling or treating Mr. Cohen as a confidential source?

A: No, I was not.

Anderson had offered convincing testimony that our witness either had lied to him or lied to the jury. Fitzmaurice also had constructed a new escape hatch for the defense. If the jury believed that Flakne had told Anderson, "I did it for Dan Cohen," then the promise of confidentiality had not been broken by the paper, but by our own witness.

Fitzmaurice had done a Perry Mason and saved his big moment for the last act. I thought that only happened on TV.

CHAPTER TWENTY-NINE

Down to the Wire

Trials are supposed to be about the search for the truth, not about trying out a series of tactics that are discarded from time to time as they become indefensible. Not this trial. We'd been through exclusivity, dirty tricks, the conundrum hypothesis, and now, the betrayed-by-his-own-witness theory.

While Fitzmaurice was examining Anderson, I was frantically searching through Anderson's book, *Investigative Reporting*, for anything we might be able to use to impeach him. I didn't find much, but it was about all we had to use against him at the moment.

Fitzmaurice objected to the use of the book, but the judge allowed it. Rothenberg cross-examined.

> Q (by Rothenberg): Mr. Anderson, in your book … you referred to something which you called "Method acting to get sources to reveal information"; is that not correct?
>
> A: (by Anderson): I hadn't read the book for a dozen years, but if you say so I believe it's in there.
>
> Q: All right. And then … you have another comment, reading as follows:
>
> If a reporter is unable to elicit sympathy from a potential source, it may be possible to inspire contempt, and the condescending carelessness that often accompanies contempt. If the source doesn't think the reporter will understand what is being said, he or she may be careless enough to answer all the reporter's questions merely to be done with it. Columbo, one of television's investigative wizards before he tripped on the

Nielson ratings consistently employs this technique. … The annoying, cross-eyed, confused look, which suggests he is paying more attention to his digestive system than to what his source is telling him would probably have netted Peter Falk two or three investigative breaks a year had he switched from acting to reporting. …

Did you say that, sir?

A: Yes.

Q: All right. Now, getting back to the testimony you gave regarding the alleged statement by Mr. Flakne which was denied by Mr. Flakne, it's true, is [it] not that there is no reference to this alleged statement by Mr. Flakne in the article itself, the rather long article?

A: No, there's none.

Q: And it's possible, is it not, that someone else had contacted Mr. Flakne, perhaps possibly one of your supervisors or one of your editors, and asked Mr. Flakne about it, and believed Mr. Flakne rather than you; is that correct, sir?

A: I would seriously doubt that. That's not the way the paper works, and if one of them ever doubted anything I said, had they thought I fabricated, I'm sure I would have heard about it.

Pretty thin stuff, but the best we could do—for the time being. Since Rothenberg hadn't finished with Finnegan, he recalled him.

Q (by Rothenberg): And then you say [in a Finnegan think piece]:

Of course, the inability of newsmen to protect their confidential sources and unpublished information will affect news gathering operations. Sources will tend to disappear. Newsmen will be suspect, seen as government informers and investigators.

The actions of many judges border on harassment and intimidation of the media. Their attitudes will stifle the free flow of information to the public. Our democracy depends on maintaining the flow.

In print, we had the fire-breathing Finnegan fulminating that the fate of the Republic hung on maintaining the confidentiality of sources.

On the witness stand, we had the avuncular Finnegan, agreeing cheerfully as Rothenberg rolled out article after article. Yes, he had written this, yes, he had written that, and then, when Hannah examined him, yes, he also supported the paper's decision to print my name.

> Q (by Hannah): Did you find any part of that decision [to publish Cohen's name] to be inconsistent with your beliefs and opinions?
>
> A (by Finnegan): No, I did not.

It was Rothenberg's turn again.

> Q (by Rothenberg): And do you recall [editorial editor Ron Clark's] testimony also that you also approved his editorial entitled "Relevant Disclosures" where the editorial position was the real story was not how the information was obtained, but that the real story was the information itself, that the information was relevant to the public, and the campaign of Perpich and Johnson could have avoided this difficulty if they—
>
> THE COURT: That's a good summary, Mr. Rothenberg.
>
> Q: The question is are you aware of that editorial, and that the editorial is, in fact, the official position of the *Pioneer Press*?
>
> A (by Finnegan): I'm aware of the editorial, and it was the position of the *Pioneer Press*.

Hannah again:

> Q (by Hannah): Mr. Finnegan, did you approve of Mr. Clark's editorial?
>
> A (by Finnegan): No, I did not.
>
> Q: Would you describe for the jury what the circumstances of that were?
>
> A: Well, in the process, I have—had direct oversight of both the news and the editorial page side, and ... under normal con-

ditions, the editorials I read prior to publication, either in text form or in the form of page proofs. The particular day in question I did not read the editorials either in the text form or page proofs prior to publication, so I found out about the editorial position the next day.

Q: Did you agree with the editorial position?

A: No, I had two disagreements with it.

Q: And what were those?

A: One was the statement that it was irrelevant whether or not Mr. Whitney knew or did not know of the information, and the second one was that inferring that the release of the information on Mr. Cohen was much less important than the release of the information on Marlene Johnson.

I did agree with the basic thrust, that the information on Marlene Johnson was important.

Rothenberg again:

Q (by Rothenberg): And you never took the opportunity, Mr. Finnegan, did you, in the columns of the *Pioneer Press*, to criticize or repudiate that editorial in any way, did you? That's correct, is it not?

A (by Finnegan): Well, not quite correct, because I did write a column the following week.

Q: But you did not specifically criticize the editorial?

A: No, I did not.

Q: And generally speaking, you mentioned, you did not disapprove that editorial before it ran, did you?

A: That's correct.

Q: And are you aware of Mr. Clark's testimony last week, sir, when Mr. Clark said that you did approve it?

MR. HANNAH: Well, I'm going to object—

THE WITNESS: I was not aware that he said he—that I approved it.

If it hadn't been lost in the middle of the Flakne/Anderson flap, Finnegan's testimony might have had more impact. As it was,

Finnegan was forced to defend himself with that feeblest of all tactics: incompetence.

Why did Finnegan, the editor of the paper, permit Clark's editorial to run when it was inconsistent with his own views on naming me as a source, which, by the way, were inconsistent with everything he had written over the years?

Because even though it was his job to read the editorials before they ran, on that particular day, he didn't do his job.

No wonder John Finnegan adopted such a beatific manner on the witness stand, while the defendants' other witnesses had fought us tooth and nail. He was good old Uncle John, the amiable bumbler. Under the circumstances, it was the best option he had.

Fitzmaurice recalled Finney. He wanted to tie Finney's decision to Anderson's testimony in order to validate their new theory that they could void their promise because they had gotten my name from an independent source. This time, Finney the Charmer gave way to the real Finney.

> Q (by Fitzmaurice): Would you explain to the members of the jury when you made the decision at 9 o'clock to go forward and identify Mr. Cohen; what it was that prompted you to make that decision?
>
> A (by Finney): Yes. First, as I've testified earlier, it was a very important subject, the information about who was releasing this information, in my judgment, was very newsworthy, as well as the information itself. So from a news point of view, I thought it was very much worthwhile to do.
>
> In addition, the information about Mr. Cohen leaving the material was becoming more and more widely known. It was part of the debate, people knew about it, and we had, from numbers of people, that they were familiar with it. And in the story we have Mr. Whitney himself referring to it. We've heard the testimony about Mr. Flakne. So we have from other sources that it was Mr. Cohen who had taken this material to the news

media. And that, in my judgment, really voided the commitment that we had made earlier to Mr. Cohen.

Q: Now, there's one other question I'd like to ask you, and that is this whole issue of exclusivity. What role, if any, did the exclusivity or lack thereof play in your decision to disclose Mr. Cohen as the source?

A: It was a factor, but it wasn't the key factor. Much more important was the fact that the story really was getting out, lots and lots of people knew about it, and beyond that, even more important, was the fact that we were able to get the information from other sources who were not bound by any commitment of confidentiality.

Cross-examination by Rothenberg:

Q (by Rothenberg): Mr. Finney, do you believe that your readers, under your analysis should have had the right to know who disclosed information claiming that Geraldine Ferraro's parents had been convicted in 1944 of gaming charges in New York?

A (by Finney): It would depend on the newsworthiness of who let that out, and I don't remember the specifics of it.

Q: And as a matter of fact, it's true is it not, sir, that there was an article very late in the campaign of 1984 in late October which referred to charges not against Ms. Ferraro and not even against her husband, but charges referring to alleged crimes of Ms. Ferraro's parents 40 years earlier on gaming charges, and those sources were not revealed; is that not correct, sir?

A: I have no ... specific recollection of that.

Q: And do you feel, sir, that your readers ought to have the right to know when charges are made three days before an election identifying the religion of a particular candidate for a School Board as being a Catholic?

A: Again, it would depend on the specific circumstances.

Q: But at least in those specific circumstances with Geraldine Ferraro and the School Board candidate, you felt, apparently, that those specific circumstances did not justify violating a promise of confidentiality to a source?

A: As I—no. As I said, I don't have any specific recollection of those.

Q: Now, regarding the issue with respect to other people, in fact, [an]other person in the article disclosed Mr. Cohen's name. In fact, Mr. Whitney—there's no reference in the article of Mr. Whitney disclosing Mr. Cohen's name, is there, sir?

A: I think he referred in the record to Mr. Cohen having the material. … Paragraph six [quoting the article]:

He [Whitney] added, "I don't recall talking to Dan Cohen in the last two months. I don't know how Dan Cohen got the information about Johnson—he must have looked it up in the records."

Q: Just a minute, sir.

A: It's vague, but it implies to me—about Cohen having had that information.

Q: In any event, there's no indication aside from your interpretation, there's no direct quote from any of these people saying—identifying Mr. Cohen as the person providing these documents, that's correct?

A: The closest is paragraph six, yes.

Q: And it's also true that neither Mr. Whitney or Mr. Olsten [his campaign manager] have been produced as witnesses to explain their statements?

A: That's true.

MR. ROTHENBERG: All right. Thank you, sir.

MR. FITZMAURICE: We rest.

And on that decidedly minor note, after ten days, the testimony in *Cohen v. Cowles Media* ended. It was Tuesday morning, July 18.

We had been able to cast very little doubt on Anderson's testimony. He and the rejuvenated Finney had given the defense a strong finishing kick. We had one last chance. That afternoon, the judge heard motions from the parties. Fitzmaurice moved for a directed verdict. This is a standard defense motion that, taking into consideration all the evidence the plaintiff has presented and even assuming that all the conflicts in the evidence were to be decided in the plaintiff's favor, the plaintiff still had not presented a case for which a valid judgment could be rendered on the basis of the law. Therefore, the jury should be directed to return a verdict for the defendants.

The heart of the defendants' legal argument was that the disclosure of my name was protected speech under the First Amendment. In their legal briefs, they cited famous cases, like *New York Times v. Sullivan* and the Larry Flynt case for the proposition that the Constitution placed a different and higher standard on those making claims against the press for breach of contract than on other plaintiffs. We argued that the First Amendment did not supercede contractual obligations, and that just because I was suing a newspaper, the law—and the cases cited by defendants—did not require me to meet a higher standard than others who claimed a breach of contract. But legal arguments are resolved by judges, not by juries, who are required to deal only with the facts.

The judge ruled in our favor, as he had earlier when the defendants made substantially the same claim in their motion for summary judgment prior to the trial. While the lawyers were arguing their motions before Judge Knoll, I stayed home and went through Anderson's book again.

Closing arguments were scheduled for the next day.

CHAPTER THIRTY

Dirty Tricks Redux

The next day the courtroom was packed. The press was there en masse as were friends and relatives of all the lawyers, dressed up as they would be for a graduation ceremony. Someone pointed out Fitzmaurice's wife, a striking blonde in a California-type print summer dress. His daughters were there, too.

Each lawyer was given an hour for a closing argument. Fitzmaurice was first.

I had expected Professor Fitzmaurice, but what we got was Tell-It-Like-It-Is Jim, a conversational, loose-limbed review of the testimony.

The theme was in the form of a question: What was the right thing to do? The subtext was: We're not on trial here. Cohen is.

He drove it home with his usual sledgehammer intensity. The answer to the question, in Fitzmaurice's view, was that on the one hand, the defendants' actions had been guided both before and after the incident by an ever-present concern over what was morally correct behavior.

On the other hand, there was my behavior.

I had not asked what the right thing to do was when I was present at the morning meeting with Flakne, nor when I cut the deal, nor when I exposed Johnson's record, nor when I, as a litigant, accused the papers of fraud and misrepresentation.

On the one hand, we had Sturdevant, who "had been a religious reporter, covering religious items" prior to covering politics. On the other hand, we have "an extremely knowledgeable person in the political arena." They had an "open agenda." We had a "secret agenda." Not only had I taken advantage of Sturdevant's naïveté, but given my experience both in politics and in the newspaper business, the jury could also draw the inference that I knew that any deal I made with Sturdevant had to be approved by her editors.

And even if there was a deal, the jury could find that the papers were free to void it because they had learned my name from an independent source.

Flakne's testimony was "disgraceful." His information about Johnson was "trash."

On the one hand, "Every single solitary editor that appeared in this trial stood on one basic proposition, and that proposition is their mission, and their aim in life is to sit down and to present news to the public that is fair and accurate."

On the other hand, "Compare that to the meeting that [was] going on. … Here were two lawyers, the head of the Republican party at one time, a professor of journalism, and they're sitting around saying how can we use this strategically?"

Why hadn't we asked ourselves, "What was the right thing to do?"

Then, one by one, Fitzmaurice went through the witnesses. Klobuchar had taken exception to my saying that Marlene Johnson and Rudy Perpich were "living a lie" when they concealed Johnson's record. "Mr. Cohen, in effect, stood up and called the Governor of this state a liar." And Mr. Klobuchar got that information and thought, "There's something wrong here, and I'm going to write a column about it." Rothenberg's attack on Klobuchar was "a little unfair. He then resurrected some old thing, I don't know what it was," for which he was suspended from the paper for making up quotes.

Grow wrote his column because "giving work outside of the workings of the University's Publicity Department and sending it to an individual who had just called the Governor of this state a liar. … It just struck him that this was a real bad idea."

196

Gelfand? "He referred to an unspoken standard. ... Basically, what it means is that ... what Mr. Cohen did was just not right. ... But he thought about it, he said, 'Well, gee, have I done it fairly?' ... He said he was troubled by what he came up with, so he thought it over some more and came back on November the 21st, 1982, and he said, 'The newspaper should be chastised, I'll chastise them because what they should have done is that they should have disclosed in the story that they ... had this on a confidential basis and that they hadn't honored that, and they should have disclosed that.'"

And so it went, witness by witness.

When mistakes were made, when there was conflict between editors, when Rothenberg produced articles showing inconsistencies between their behavior in this case and their behavior in other cases, it all could be explained—if the jury would just keep in mind that the defendants were always asking themselves, "What was the right thing to do?"—and that time after time I had failed to ask myself the same question. Fitzmaurice closed:

> Mr. Cohen did not come into this courtroom with a single shred of compassion, in my view, or feelings of sorrow or regret or any human emotion as far as Marlene Johnson is concerned. And I'm not angry about that. I find it sad. ... He has not shown one single ounce of regret for this terrible act that's the subject of this lawsuit.

He got in a little opprobrium, too, and infamy, and very sneaky stuff. Dirty tricks had the day off, but it was very much present in spirit. The word *exclusivity* did not cross his lips.

When he got to the damages, he said that "if you find that there was a breach of this contract and that damages are owed to Mr. Cohen, the appropriate amount of money is $20,000, as opposed to $227,000 which is arrived at by taking all of these numbers that bear no relationship." I was surprised he even conceded the possibility we might win.

It was an old-fashioned horse opera. Marlene Johnson was the damsel in distress. The newspaper was the hero, riding to her rescue. I got the black hat.

Fitzmaurice had so many points to make, both on offense and defense, that the central theme got lost from time to time in all the digressions. But he always got back to it, with the terrible act coda at the end, true to its melodramatic origins.

Hannah was next.

His choice of a theme was the strange hook metaphor he had foreshadowed in his opening remarks. A hook was an important event. The meeting with Flakne and Co. was a hook. Hannah's description of the meeting added little to what Fitzmaurice had said:

> The second hook, the decision by the papers to run the story. ... You heard Mr. Hall describe the reason for his decision. That is, it was around [widely known], it wasn't confidential, and besides, there was something more here than just a story about Marlene Johnson. ... [There was] a difficult, but I think straightforward and honest decision by Mr. Hall. Innocence and honesty don't equal fraud and misrepresentation.

Hannah punted on damages: "I submit that any loss Mr. Cohen suffered came from his own voluntary participation in an attempt to hurt Marlene Johnson's campaign, and I would further submit that harm does not come from an article that is, in essence, true."

Hannah went over the article in the St. Paul paper at some length, quoting the paragraph that named me, which read, "Dan Cohen, a Minneapolis advertising and public relations consultant, gave the court records to at least three reporters but asked that his name not be used."

"I would submit that that was a fair article." Hannah said. "And further, I would submit that given the obvious fairness of this article to seek punitive damages in this case from the defendants who worked as hard as they did during that day to bring these facts to light, is preposterous."

That was it for Hannah. He made no attempt to refute our most damaging testimony against them: his paper's editorial position supporting my disclosure of Johnson's record and Finnegan's own description of revealing an anonymous source as a dirty trick. He even had aped Fitzmaurice's use of the word *preposterous* to describe the claim for punitive damages for fraud and misrepresentation.

Rothenberg was next, and last. His theme was a promise made and a promise broken. Who were the defendants? he asked. Not Finney or McGuire, but "two enormous media giants":

> Most of [the defendants'] case was a diatribe, a personal attack against Mr. Cohen, talking about [the] infamy of Mr. Cohen and other words of that sort. And what was this so-called infamy of Mr. Cohen? All Mr. Cohen had done, as you know from the testimony in this case, is [provide] copies of authentic court records to reporters from the *Star & Tribune*, the *Pioneer Press Dispatch*, WCCO-TV and the Associated Press.

Rothenberg again quoted extensively from the "Relevant Disclosures" editorial that had appeared in the St. Paul papers and described it as "probably the most important document in this case regarding the position of the two newspapers." It says,

> To focus on how the information got to the public's attention is to overlook a larger issue; that is, the information about the Lieutenant Governor candidate, Marlene Johnson, is something the public deserves to know. ... It is legitimate to examine her fitness for public office. ... The last-minute disclosure could have been avoided if Mr. Perpich and Ms. Johnson had informed the public themselves earlier and confronted the issue squarely.

Rothenberg then focused on Gelfand's testimony, which had shown that "the real issue is ... not some sort of phony moral issue about providing copies of valid and authentic court documents, but merely the fact that … [one newspaper] did not have a commercial advantage over its competitor. … They wanted to have a scoop on it, they wanted to have it exclusively, and because they didn't have it exclusively, didn't have a scoop, they engaged in what is a vendetta against Mr. Cohen for the past six years, and don't you believe it's anything but that. … What did Mr. Nimmer say about the motives of the newspapers involved here? The words were 'Dan Cohen was hung out to dry by the newspapers because they didn't like him.'"

Next were Sturdevant and Salisbury who "wouldn't testify on behalf of the newspapers because they were so opposed and they were so angry that their word was being broken. … They testified for Mr. Cohen in this case. … Ms. Sturdevant said that she had dealt with Mr. Cohen in the past. … She knew that he was working on the Whitney campaign. … Not only that, but she had also given Mr. Cohen a promise of confidentiality on another matter, a promise which was kept. … She was so angry that her promise of confidentiality was being violated, being dishonored, she didn't want to have anything to do with that article. It was an unethical act, an immoral act."

Then there was the conundrum hypothesis, the defendants' argument that when it came to telling the truth, they had to choose between me and their readers. "They said they … wanted to be complete and level with the public. … That article, which was purportedly complete was very incomplete in one major respect. It did not disclose that the information had been obtained in return for a promise of confidentiality to him, it did not disclose that newspapers had dishonored the promise of their reporters to him, and it did not disclose that the person who wrote the article, Lori Sturdevant, was so angry at that decision that she refused to allow her name to be used on that article." The papers had been no more truthful in dealing with their readers than they had been in dealing with me.

"We're talking about an agreement between Mr. Cohen and four different reporters to provide information in exchange for a promise that his name will not be disclosed as a source of that information," Rothenberg continued. "Mr. Nimmer kept his promise ... and the same with Gerry Nelson, ... who now works for the Perpich administration. ... He also worked for Marlene Johnson. ... We've asked editors, we've asked experts, and no one has been able to point to a [case] in the entire country where a promise of confidentiality to a source by a reporter has been voluntarily broken and dishonored by the editors of a newspaper."

And so it went, witness after witness, the same technique Fitzmaurice had used.

There's a saying students learn their first week in law school: those who seek relief in equity must have clean hands. When you accuse the opposing party of dirty tricks, you'd better not be guilty of having committed a dirty trick yourself.

Klobuchar had been suspended from the papers for making up quotes, and then, a few months after the article about me appeared, he was again suspended "for failing to make full disclosure, for failing to level with the public" when he secretly helped write Perpich's inaugural speech. No clean hands there.

"What did Doug Grow say to Mr. Konrath?" Rothenberg continued. "That was after the election, after Mr. Cohen was humiliated. It wasn't enough. Doug Grow said, 'Why in the world would you hire anybody like Dan Cohen?' Apparently Dan Cohen isn't supposed to get a job anywhere, according to newspapers. ... But the capper came [from] something else. Remember we asked Doug Grow how did he find out that Dan Cohen was working for the University of Minnesota? And what did Doug Grow say? 'I found out from a confidential source and I've kept the name of that confidential source secret for these years, and I'm not going to tell you right now the name of that confidential source.'

"Well, is this a dirty trick? Was this a dirty trick, trying to sabotage the job and position which Dan Cohen was able to get? Nobody in the *Star & Tribune* said, 'Well, Mr. Grow, you've got to identify that source, he's maligning Dan Cohen, he's committing an act of infamy against Dan Cohen.'"

No clean hands there, either.

"There was a dirty trick here," Rothenberg went on, "and the dirty trick, as Mr. Finnegan pointed out in his testimony yesterday, was not providing copies of authentic court records to newspaper reporters for them to do as they will, but the dirty trick was a violation of a promise of confidentiality to a source. That's what Mr. Finnegan says in the article which you will have before you, that the violation of a promise of confidentiality to a source is a dirty trick.

"Those are the words of a former editor-in-chief of the *St. Paul Pioneer Press* which is a party in this case, those are the words of the current vice president of the *St. Paul Pioneer Press*, those are the words he repeated before you yesterday and which he said again he agrees with. So much for dirty tricks in this case. You know, the last gasp of the *Star & Tribune* was to bring in their last witness yesterday, a gentleman by the name of David Anderson, where he now says after all this time that they didn't break a promise because the information was actually gotten from Gary Flakne and not from Cohen, Mr. Cohen. But I'm sure that would be news for Lori Sturdevant or Bill Salisbury or to Roger Buoen or to the others who have been involved in this case. In fact, you will read the article from the *Star & Tribune* and the *Pioneer Press Dispatch*. There is no reference to any allusion or any allusion that this information was provided independently by Mr. Flakne.

"It's ridiculous."

"And you know, there's a reference to the book by Mr. Anderson called *Investigative Reporting*. Just to read you an excerpt as we did yesterday, this is what he said,

> Many fundamental techniques of investigative reporting involve actions some would label dishonest, fraudulent, immoral, and perhaps even illegal. Most reporters use deceptive methods to gather information.

"That's Mr. Anderson. That's the gentleman they are putting on the stand to say they did not ... get this information from reporters ... rather from Mr. Flakne. You can assess the credibility of that, too, ladies and gentlemen of the jury.

"The issue in this case, ladies and gentlemen, is not attacks on the character of Mr. Cohen. That's an attempt to divert you from the real issues. You can decide for yourselves when you've last heard attacks on an individual as vicious as those that have been leveled at Mr. Cohen in this case by attorneys in this case. The issue really is this, ladies and gentlemen: are the rules of morality, contract, honoring one's word, the ethics of persons, a man or woman's word being his or her bond, the legal rules of keeping one's agreements, rules which all of us as individuals want to live by and are required to live by, are those rules also going to bind the huge corporate entities representing the newspapers that are involved in this suit?

"If they're able to evade their obligations by instead of arguing on the basis of law to attack the character of the individual who is suing them, all contracts will be at risk. No one will be safe. No individual will be safe in this type of situation.

"And it's not only done in this type of case either, ladies and gentlemen of the jury. This is a common tactic of defendants in rape cases to attack the character of the victim, the woman raped, rather than dealing with the true issues involved in that case. ... We ask you to enforce the morality, basic morality which governs all of us, of keeping one's word as your bond. That's the basis of the law, that's the basis of journalistic ethics.

"We ask you, members of the jury, to give justice to Dan Cohen and to restore to him and his family his good name, so that we can throw this cartoon into oblivion where it belongs."

Over the top? Rothenberg had out-Fitzmauriced Fitzmaurice. Had the defense been hoist by their own petard? Maybe.

CHAPTER THIRTY-ONE

The Verdict

The next day the judge gave the jury its instructions. Judge Knoll overruled Fitzmaurice's objections to the use of Anderson's book—where I finally found what I was looking for—and to Rothenberg's reference to rape. Two white-knuckled days later, on Friday, July 22, we were called back to the courtroom. The jury had returned with a verdict.

When we got there, there was a new face in the courtroom: an armed county sheriff. Whose idea was that? Was he there to mow me down in case I pulled out a gun and tried to pop Fitzmaurice if the verdict went against me?

Fitzmaurice was safe.

The jury awarded me $200,000 for breach of contract, and an additional $250,000 in punitive damages from each defendant for fraud and misrepresentation. The total was $700,000.

I hugged Gail, hugged Rothenberg, hugged Gail and Rothenberg, and went over to the jury box and thanked each of the jurors, minus the hug-a-thon. It was a five-to-one verdict. One of the two male jurors had dissented. I didn't know who it was, but as I reached to shake the last hand, the sixth juror turned away and left the courtroom. Fitzmaurice and Hannah were standing at the defendant's table. I shook hands with each of them, but we had nothing to say to each other.

The press was waiting in the atrium of the courthouse. Other than my testimony, I had not made a public statement about the incident since the day I handed over Marlene Johnson's record to the defendants.

For ten years, the defendants had been heaping me with garbage—in their own milieu, the media—and now, a jury of their peers had decided, in an unbiased forum, a court of law, that they, not I, had engaged in fraud and misrepresentation.

Fraud and misrepresentation. Like Jim Bakker, the televangelist, who was doing time in the federal pen a hundred miles away for bilking his gullible viewers out of millions of dollars. Like Ivan Boesky and Michael Milken, the junk-bond kings.

Fraud and misrepresentation. Like common criminals. Plain old liars.

They had tried to use their enormous power to crush me and, by example, to deter anyone else who would challenge their hegemony over the known world. Instead, they had left the courtroom branded liars and frauds by the very same people who read the words they wrote in their papers every day.

I was waylaid by the media as I walked through the lobby of the courthouse, and I made a brief statement. "Keeping one's word is the hard currency of journalism. And it's the hard currency of politics. And it's the hard currency of human existence. When hard currency is devalued, we all suffer." About as bland as you can get and still have something to say besides "no comment."

McGuire spoke for the *Star Tribune*. He was "shocked." He told the *New York Times* that it was disturbing to see an oral agreement between a reporter and a source treated like "a contract to sell paper clips. ... There should be a higher standard than whether or not a reporter made a promise to a source." Finnegan was "shocked," too. He put his special spin on matters by emphasizing, in a television interview, that the verdict had not been unanimous.

Mary Catherine Fuller, a suburban librarian, was the forewoman of the jury. When the *Star Tribune* interviewed her, she said that the *Star Tribune* could have served their readers just as well by identifying me simply as a Whitney supporter:

> But [Fuller] said neither the ethics of the editors' decision to print Cohen's name nor the ethics of Cohen's election-eve disclosure entered into the panel's decision.
>
> "We were not there to judge the morals or practices of journalism. The question was: What is the law and what happened in this case?"

Each side's name-calling had cancelled the other's. The jury had tuned it all out, and followed the judge's instructions. There was a contract. The papers had breached it and done it with willful indifference, hence, fraud and misrepresentation:

> The forewoman compared the situation to a highway speeder who claims he does not know the speed limit. She said the newspapers had a responsibility to inform their reporters of policies limiting their authority.

When *Time* magazine reported on the case, it quoted Bill Kennedy, Hennepin County public defender, and a Democrat: "This is a very simple case. A promise is a promise."

The article also reported a further development:

> Many reporters and editors at the papers had seen the Cohen case as an aberration. But even before the verdict was read, the *Star Tribune* faced the threat of a new breach-of-contract suit. Freelance Writer Martha Thomas sold an article to the paper's *Sunday* magazine telling the inside story of a rape trial. Thomas interviewed the defense lawyer on condition that her name not appear. But *Star Tribune* editors insisted that, because the trial was open to the public, it was fair to name names. Late last week the newspaper pulled all 625,000 copies of its *Sunday* magazine rather than risk litigation. Considering Cohen's victory, that seemed a prudent move.

It wasn't just the *Star Tribune* and *Time* that were dissecting the case. So did the local PBS TV station on its weekly political program, *Almanac*. Rothenberg appeared, but no one from either of the papers did. Under the circumstances, they preferred media venues where we didn't show up. The moderator/commentator, a woman who later ran as, yes, the Democratic candidate for lieutenant governor, asked Rothenberg if we weren't guilty of "beating up" on the press. No. it would be pretty tough for two guys to beat up on a couple of billion-dollar media companies.

The national PBS TV news program *The McNeil/Lehrer Report* did a half-hour roundtable that featured McGuire and three other journalists in a hand-holding session. We were not asked to appear. One of the press mavens had the guts to observe that he regarded the *Star Tribune's* behavior as "unprofessional" but, nonetheless, wished McGuire well in his crusade to preserve "freedom of the press."

In the weeks that followed, the papers had a new object of unaffection. They criticized Judge Knoll publicly for his failure to throw the case out on First Amendment grounds.

Never one to take an unanswered blow, Judge Knoll responded in his courtroom when the papers appeared on August 22 for oral argument on their motions for a judgment notwithstanding the verdict or, alternatively, for a new trial.

> THE COURT: In the support of accuracy in journalism, I think it should be noted that the orders of the Court and the rulings on the motions ... in no way affects the newspaper's right to publish what it wants to publish, short of libel or slander, and the order of the Court merely applies to the newspaper when it chooses to publish, the same law that applies to any other citizen, namely, the law of contracts and the law of torts. ... I think that for the company to continue stating publicly that this Court's order in some way impinges on its right to publish is erroneous.

This admonition was, of course, lost on the papers, since being erroneous was a concept that applied to others. Besides, the papers were in an all-out sulk. Judge Knoll denied their motions in a written opinion issued on November 19.

He dismissed their arguments about flagrant misconduct in Rothenberg's closing statement to the jury. Judge Knoll wrote, "If anything, closing arguments by *all* counsel were emotionally charged." He went on to describe their actions by saying, "Certainly, the knowing and willful breach of a legally sufficient contract after hours of thought and discussion by corporate officers can fairly be characterized as a 'calculated misdeed.'" Calculated misdeed. Fraud and misrepresentation. Elegant versions of dirty tricks.

That was the papers' last gasp in district court. Naturally, they appealed.

CHAPTER THIRTY-TWO

Court of Last Resort

Seven hundred thousand dollars is a lot of money. Particularly when it's out there just beyond reach. The defendants didn't have to pay us—yet. They could post a bond for the money, the civil equivalent of posting bail for your own sweet body in a criminal case. I waived the posting requirement in return for a partial payment of my expenses. They weren't about to leave town or go broke. They saved money. I saved money. It's amazing how people who hated each other as much as the parties to this lawsuit did could still do business, when we could both save a few bucks.

As for the big money, Rothenberg and I got into a dispute over the $700,000 we didn't have. Our original deal had been a typical contingency agreement, "to represent you in your litigation" in return for "one-third of the net recovery from this litigation."

But on October 5, Rothenberg wrote me: "I have given you the option of compensating me for my services in the appeal process either by an increase in the contingency rate from one-third to 40 percent or by the contingency rate plus an hourly fee for services related to the appeal or appeals. You have told me that you refuse to provide any compensation for these services other than what you previously agreed to pay for my handling of your trial."

That's right. I refused. According to *Black's Law Dictionary*, *litigation* means not just the trial, but "legal action, including all proceedings therein." That includes the appeals. A deal is a deal, whether it's with the papers or it's with the lawyer I hired to sue the papers. What was it that made everybody think they could retrade their deals with me?

Success can be as corrosive to a relationship as failure. Both Rothenberg and I had experienced too much of the latter to know how to handle the former. But I didn't want to lose him. I needed to find an avuncular type who could set Rothenberg straight without offending him so much he'd walk. I hired another lawyer, Frank Berman. Both Rothenberg and I knew and liked him.

Berman did some legal research, pointed out to Rothenberg that he was in danger of losing not only his client, but also his claim to any fee whatsoever, and the firestorm passed as quickly as it had started.

Rothenberg reaffirmed our original agreement, resumed being his old gracious self, and *Cohen v. Cowles* marched on.

Next stop: the Minnesota Court of Appeals.

As previously reported, judges are lawyers who know a governor. District court judges also know the custom of the area where they hold court. A Minneapolis pol like Frank Knoll who becomes a Minneapolis trial judge has a good working knowledge of the realities of dealing with the gentlefolk at the *Minneapolis Star Tribune*.

Not necessarily so with appellate judges. They can come from anywhere in the state. Despite Minnesota's pretensions as an island of sophistication in the midst of flyover land, there's a lot of uncharted territory out there. Thus, one court of appeals judge, Gary Crippen, a lawyer from Worthington, population 9,977 (a city of the "fourth class" under Minnesota law, so small that it can maintain a municipal liquor store without a vote of the citizens) wrote, in his opinion:

> To accomplish his ends, respondent chose not to approach the editors who would be expected to make publication decisions. He chose not to make his proposal in a deliberative setting.

> Instead, he approached reporters on their beat, expecting he
> might readily arouse in them some desire for nuggets of politi-
> cal news. ... He neither sought nor obtained a deliberative
> pledge of anonymity by media editors.

Maybe when someone wants to be an anonymous source at
the *Worthington Daily Globe* (circulation 13,250), they sit down
"in a deliberative setting" with a kindly old editor and thrash out
an understanding, but I don't recall Arnold Ismach, the dean of
the School of Journalism at the University of Oregon, suggesting
to me that's how you do a deal with the *Minneapolis Star Tribune.*
Judge Crippen also failed to mention that I carefully went over
the material with both reporters—each of whom deliberated
long enough to express some enthusiasm over what I had given
them—in exchange for their promises.

Anyway, Judge Crippen's opinion was a dissent. On
September 5, 1989, a little over a year after the jury trial, the
Minnesota Court of Appeals voted 2–1 to affirm the district
court judgment on the contract portion of the verdict, holding
that our claim did not restrict freedom of the press and therefore
did not implicate the First Amendment; and further, that even if
the First Amendment were involved, the papers had waived their
rights when they made their deal with me. But they unanimously reversed our judgment for fraud and misrepresentation. The
papers didn't commit fraud because to be actionable, "a misrepresentation must misrepresent a present or past fact." The
reporters I dealt with didn't lie. They had every intention of performing the contract. They actually thought they had a deal. I
conceded that in my testimony, and as a matter of law, that was
fatal to our claim of fraud and misrepresentation.

Our $700,000 pie in the sky had been reduced to a $200,000
slice. But the papers could never reverse the fact that a jury of
their peers had branded them as liars.

Both parties appealed to the Minnesota Supreme Court. We appealed the reversal of the fraud and misrepresentation claim; they appealed the remaining judgment for breach of contract.

Though Fitzmaurice's name appeared on the briefs for the *Star Tribune*, he made no further courtroom appearances. I ran into him once about a year after the trial. It was at the grocery store on a Saturday morning, and he was wearing a sweatshirt with a logo from Georgetown, his law school. No glasses on a strap. We still had nothing to say to each other.

By this time, the tone of the briefs and the oral arguments had taken on a formal, legalistic tone. This was not lawyers talking to juries. This was lawyers talking to lawyers. We talked about contracts. The papers talked about the First Amendment. Neither side waved the bloody flag. The tactical arguments, like dirty tricks and rape, were subsumed in discussions of legal concepts. The misadventures of Miss Minnesota USA gave way to dull case law like *Guy T. Bisbee Co. v. Granite City Investing Corp.*

The Minnesota Supreme Court presented us with a bit of a problem. Before Rudy Perpich appointed him to the bench, the chief justice, Peter Popovich, had been a state senator from the Iron Range, just like his buddy, Perpich. Reading Judge Popovich's previous opinions, it was clear he was not going to come down on our side. Popovich had also, at one time, been a lawyer for the *St. Paul Pioneer Press.* We wanted him off the case. What to do? Rule one: you never publicly embarrass or criticize a sitting judge. Not only does it piss off the judge you're dissing, it also pisses off all the other judges who may have a say in your case. The judge club is tighter than Skull and Bones. The surest way to lose an appeal is to claim that the lower court judge had some personal bias.

Here we had a situation in which we had ample grounds to claim that the chief justice of the state had a potential conflict of interest. If we said so in public, he might step down, but the other supreme court judges would quietly sharpen their knives for us.

So, when we filed our briefs, Rothenberg privately wrote a letter to Chief Justice Popovich asking him to recuse himself because of his prior connection to one of the defendants. He never answered the letter.

On the day of the oral arguments, we were standing just outside the courtroom, when Popovich popped up, in his robes, and gestured to Rothenberg he wanted to speak with him privately.

"What did he say?" I asked Rothenberg.

"He says he isn't going to say anything. He isn't going to ask any questions or participate in the decision, but he wants to sit on the bench and hear the case. He also says he could have decided the case fairly."

"What did you say?"

"What could I say? If that's what he wants to do, that's what he's going to do."

Popovich sat silently on the bench while the rest of the judges peppered the attorneys with questions. Justice Rosalie Wahl, another Perpich appointee and the first woman to be appointed to the Minnesota Supreme Court, asked Rothenberg why we hadn't just slipped the documents under the door in an unmarked envelope. My favorite question.

"Because plaintiff thought he could trust the *Minneapolis Star and Tribune* and the *St. Paul Pioneer Press* to keep their word."

She voted against us.

On July 20, 1990, the Minnesota Supreme Court filed its opinion. The decision went four to two in favor of the defendants. The court not only upheld the dismissal of the fraud and misrepresentation charge, but reversed the remaining portion of the verdict that had awarded us $200,000 on the contract claim.

Justice John Simonett, writing for the court, said:

> The court must balance the constitutional rights of a free press against the common law interest in protecting a promise of anonymity. ... It seems to us that the law best leaves the parties here to their trust in each other. What you have here, it seems

to us, is an "I'll-scratch-your-back-if-you'll-scratch-mine" accommodation. Each party, we think, assumes the risks of what might happen.

There were two separate dissents. Justice Lawrence Yetka wrote:

> I find the consequences of this decision deplorable. ... The decision sends out a clear message that if you are wealthy and powerful enough, the law simply does not apply to you. ... It is unconscionable to allow the press, on the one hand, to hide behind the shield of confidentiality when it does not want to reveal the source of the information, yet, on the other hand, to violate confidentiality agreements with impunity when it decides that disclosing the source will make its story more sensational and profitable.

In his dissent, Justice Richard Kelly underlined "the perfidy of these defendants, the liability for which they now seek to escape by crawling under the aegis of the First Amendment, which in my opinion has nothing to do with the case."

That was it.

All I had to show for eight years of humiliation and litigation was a now-defunct jury verdict and some strong judicial language about the defendants' character. Cold comfort. No fraud or misrepresentation. No contract. No nothing.

The Associated Press, which filed the only friend-of-the-court brief in the case, had taken a position totally at odds with the behavior of Gerry Nelson, the AP reporter who had kept his word to me. Their attorneys praised the decision as one from which the news media "can take considerable comfort."

Hannah's comment was that it was important that the court recognized the very special relationship between a reporter and source.

We had only one shot left.

The United States Supreme Court hears only 2 percent of the cases presented to it on writs of certiorari, the only route that was available to us. The odds were 50 to 1 against us.

The time had come to let Rothenberg know how much I valued him—now when we were down, not when we were up.

"Elliot, remember my saying I don't want to retrade our deal?"

"I surely do."

"Well, I want to retrade our deal. Unilaterally. You've done a hell of a job. I want to raise your cut to 40 percent."

Rothenberg then did what Rothenberg did best: he immersed himself in the stacks of the Hennepin County Law Library for two months, got the job done, and beat the odds. On December 20, 1990, the United States Supreme Court granted certiorari.

John Borger, an attorney with Fitzmaurice's firm who had made the oral argument for the *Star Tribune* in the court of appeals and the Minnesota Supreme Court, had said earlier, "We basically believe that any further review by any court is likely to accept the analysis employed by the Minnesota Supreme Court."

He was whistling past the graveyard. The United States Supreme Court does not accept cases from lesser forums in order to give them their stamp of approval. Lyle Deniston, who wrote a regular column for the *Washington Journalism Review*, had it right:

> Already, lawyers who defend the press are deep in agony over the mere fact that the court was willing to hear that case. They anticipate a major constitutional defeat. Said one of those worried lawyers in private (with some exaggeration for effect): "It's the end of the world!"

There go those anonymous sources again. I wonder who that one was.

CHAPTER THIRTY-THREE

End Game

Gail and I went to Washington to hear the oral argument. It was March 27, 1991, the first time I'd been back since I had worked for the Peace Corps over a decade earlier. My old office with a view of the White House, in a six-story building on Lafayette Square, was gone, replaced by a new office, with more stories and more views of the White House. My old watering hole, the Café de François, was gone, too, mercifully. I'd stopped drinking there the evening I saw a Norway rat the size of a Humvee scamper in the front door. Though I'd lived in Washington and done the usual tourist bit, I had never seen the United States Supreme Court building. When I got there I knew why. The building is small, tired, and in a bad part of town. When we were getting out of the cab, I gave the driver an extra twenty dollars.

"We're going to be getting out of here at exactly 11 o'clock. I'd like to have you waiting right here to pick us up."

I didn't care to get trapped by reporters while I was trying to flag down a non-existent cab. I'd save my comments for the day the decision came out.

You need tickets to get into this show. Ours had come in the mail about a month earlier. There was no assigned seating. We stood in line for a while and then we were marched into the gallery, single file, filling up the seats in the order in which we entered the room. I knew the drill. I used to do it every morning at military school when we had auditorium.

In addition to the briefs submitted by the parties, friend-of-the-court briefs on behalf of the papers had been filed by Advance Publications, the American Newspaper Publishers Association, the American Society of Newspaper Editors, the Associated Press, the Copley Press, Inc., the Gannett Company, Inc., the Newsletter Association, the New York Times Company, and the Times Mirror Company.

No friend-of-the-court briefs were filed on our behalf.

Each side had half an hour to argue their case. The Court does not have a high tolerance for oratorical flights of fancy. There were questions and more questions.

Once again, Rothenberg was asked why I hadn't just passed the document in an unmarked envelope. Once again, he responded that "Mr. Cohen, as many other confidential sources, felt that he could trust the promises of the reporters." And once again, the questioner was the Court's single female justice—who voted against us. The defendants' oral argument was made by John French, a longtime activist in Minnesota's Democratic Party. His adversary, as it happened, was none other than Justice Thurgood Marshall, the first black ever to serve on the U.S. Supreme Court.

> MR. FRENCH: If this Court's decisions protect under the First Amendment the utterance of defamatory speech, surely this Court must find some room under the First Amendment to protect the utterance of honest, accurate speech.
>
> QUESTION (by Justice Marshall): Mr. French, on that word "honest," did you publish that you promised not to publish that?
>
> MR. FRENCH: The two reporters gave Mr. Cohen a promise that they wouldn't—
>
> QUESTION: Did you publish that the deal was made not to release it?
>
> MR. FRENCH: They, did not, Your Honor.
>
> QUESTION: Well, now you're talking about truth. You didn't publish the truth.

> MR. FRENCH: The entire truth about everything did not
> get published.
> QUESTION: You didn't publish all the truth.

After all these years, the defining moment. Thurgood Marshall always supported First Amendment claims by the press. When, like the old pols we were, Rothenberg and I had tried to count noses, we hadn't counted his to be one of the five votes we needed. Marshall was within a few months of retirement. He wasn't going to make a deathbed conversion and join the conservatives of the Rehnquist court by voting against the press. We knew that. No matter. He had cut through the clutter. You don't bullshit Thurgood Marshall.

I was elated. And ashamed. Thurgood Marshall, of all people. The last person on the Court from whom I expected—or deserved—any support. I had been indifferent—at best—to the concerns of black people my entire life, and here was the first black person to serve on the United States Supreme Court, saving my ass.

When the oral arguments were over, we dashed out of the courtroom, pursued by the press. As we crossed in front of the building, headed for our loyally waiting cab, we passed Deborah Howell standing on the courthouse steps, spinning a covey of rapt reporters.

On June 25, 1991, in a five-to-four decision, the United States Supreme Court ruled in our favor, holding that the First Amendment did not bar my action against these papers. It was close to a pure ideological split. We got Chief Justice William Rehnquist, Antonin Scalia, Anthony Kennedy, Byron White, and John Paul Stevens. They got Sandra Day O'Connor, Marshall, Harry Blackmun, and the stealth liberal, David Souter.

Justice White delivered the opinion of the Court:

> The First Amendment does not confer on the press a constitutional right to disregard promises that would otherwise be

enforced under state law. The press has no "special immunity" from observing general laws and "no special privilege to invade the rights and liberties of others."

Blackmun, dissenting, wrote that the papers should not be penalized for publishing "truthful" information. Souter joined him, claiming that the papers had the right to publish my name because it "expanded the universe of choice faced by Minnesota voters."

For the *Star Tribune*, it was spin time as usual. "We are pleased that four of the nine justices recognized that, in making the difficult decision to overrule a promise of confidentiality made to a source, we served vital public interests by providing important information to the electorate on the eve of an election," said Randy Lebedoff, general counsel of the *Star Tribune*.

The word from the *Pioneer Press* was much the same. "We are disappointed in the U.S. Supreme Court's ruling. Nonetheless, we trust the state's highest court will reaffirm its earlier decision," said Mary Junck, speaking for the St. Paul papers as publisher and president.

I had a few comments, too: "The newspapers' attempts to wrap themselves in the First Amendment and their politicization of the case has brought them to ruin. ... They have humiliated themselves nationally and humiliated the profession. ... Thanks to their arrogance and stupidity, the *Minneapolis Star Tribune* and the *St. Paul Pioneer Press* are now nationally certified as liars."

The case now went back to the Minnesota Supreme Court. Unknown to most people, including me, an alleged lawyer, the United States Supreme Court is not a court where you enter judgment. They do what they do, then send the cases back to where they came from for action consistent with their decision.

And what had they decided? Basically, only that the papers' First Amendment arguments didn't protect them from my claims of breach of contract. They still had all their other defenses.

However, by this time, the Minnesota Supreme Court had had enough and reversed their original decision. In an opinion filed on January 24, 1992, the Minnesota Supreme Court ruled unanimously that the papers had made a legally enforceable promise to me. Justice Simonett wrote that it was significant that the papers' editors had testified that they believed that promises of confidentiality must "generally" be honored. "It was this long-standing journalistic tradition that Cohen, who has worked in journalism, relied upon in asking for and receiving a promise of anonymity."

The spin doctors at the papers had just about run out of yarn. Speaking for the *Star Tribune*, Tim McGuire had a one-line statement, "We are obviously disappointed in the decision, but we respect it."

Hannah was just as brief. "The only official comment is our disappointment at the results."

I was, admittedly, a bit nasty. "The message of this case is clear. Minnesota juries and courts will not protect intentional lies by even those as rich, powerful, and politically correct as the *Minneapolis Star Tribune* and the *St. Paul Pioneer Press*."

The final act came in July 1992, when the defendants contested our claims for interest on the judgment. By this time, four years after the jury verdict, with $200,000 remaining on the judgment, interest and interest on the interest had reached $131,000.

An arcane Minnesota statute provided that interest was computed on whichever amount proposed as a settlement by either party was closest to the figure the jury had arrived at. The written settlement figure closest to that amount—in fact, the only written settlement offer—was the $4,000 I had rejected when Charlie Hvass had represented me. Obviously, interest on $4,000 was not $131,000. It was nominal.

The Minnesota Supreme Court, in sending the case back down to the district court, had hinted broadly that the controlling case law favored the defendants' argument that interest should be computed on the $4,000.

However, the defendants' written offer of $4,000 also included a proposed statement to be made public by the parties that said I had received no money.

Throughout the life of this case, the defendants had claimed that their readers had the right to know the truth.

But their concept of the truth had not impressed Thurgood Marshall.

Or the majority on the United States Supreme Court.

Or, eventually, the Minnesota Supreme Court.

Or the Minnesota Court of Appeals.

Or, Frank Knoll, the trial judge.

Or the jury.

And certainly not us.

There, in their own settlement proposal, in writing, was a lie they had prepared for public consumption.

They were to give me $4,000 and I was to say I had received no money.

When the defendants saw our brief, they dropped their claims on interest.

The final scene was played out in one of those anonymous downtown glass block office buildings where I was to receive—and sign for—the checks.

I told Rothenberg I wanted to walk into the room, sign my name to whatever piece of paper got stuck in front of me, take the check, and then we would walk out together. No chitchat. No reminiscences. No thank-yous. No farewells. No dining-out stories for the defendants' lawyers.

When I got there, Rothenberg had tipped my hand.

"I've got it all taken care of, Dan. Everything is in order. All you have to do is sign the paper and we can leave."

The defendants' lawyers looked at me with bemused tolerance. They already had their dining-out stories; I had tried to convert an ordinary business meeting into a solemn ceremony, à la the Japanese surrender on the USS *Missouri*.

The pen didn't work, either. I had to get another one.

I signed the paper. They handed us the check. I was paid the full amount, the $200,000 judgment and the $131,000 of interest and interest on interest up to the exact date on which I received payment. "Going to the bank now?" said Hannah.

"Yeah," I said.

That was the end of *Cohen v. Cowles*, but not the end of the story.

Throughout the years, I've thought a lot about what happened. For a long time, I couldn't write about it. I couldn't face reading again what the papers had said about me. I needed time and space to heal.

I also needed distance so that whatever I wrote wouldn't be as much a polemic as a reasonably balanced narrative.

But still, one question has nagged at me over all these years and I still do not know the answer: on the morning I went to see Lori Sturdevant and Bill Salisbury, had they already heard about Johnson's arrest record?

I don't see how a part-time talk show host like Dick Pomerantz, who juggled issues from abortion to gun control to state politics, could be better informed about Johnson than experienced reporters for the state's two major metropolitan dailies who had been assigned full-time to cover the gubernatorial election. If Sturdevant and Salisbury hadn't heard about Johnson, then not only was Pomerantz better informed than they were, so were the thousands of his listeners who had heard about it on the radio. And so was Nimmer, who had told me that "this stuff had been kicking around a couple of days."

It just doesn't make sense.

As I was leaving her office that morning, Sturdevant had said to me, "Come by any time you have material like this." What she hadn't said was, "I was surprised to see this material." And neither had Salisbury. If they hadn't known about it, they should have been surprised. And when people are surprised, they tend to say so. Yet if the reporters had heard about it, why hadn't they checked on it? Why had Flakne been the first person in years to dig up Johnson's record from the catacombs?

My guess is, the reporters had known about it and either hadn't regarded it as important enough to bother with or had told their editors, and their editors had told them it wasn't important enough to bother with.

If I'm right, then our whole case, both legally and in terms of the motivation of the papers' editors, takes on a new dimension.

If the reporters had heard about Johnson before we cut the deal, then there was no contract. In legal terms, they had received no consideration, consideration being something of value, in return for their promise to me. What I gave them, they already had. When there's no consideration, there's no contract.

But there was fraud. That's because even though they hadn't lied, they had knowingly misled me. They knew I thought at the time they didn't know about Johnson, and this is what induced me to make the exchange: their promise for my documents.

Our two theories of liability, breach of contract and fraud, were legally incompatible. If it's a contract, then there's a meeting of the minds, both parties agree upon the essential elements of the deal. Like consideration, a meeting of the minds is a necessary ingredient of any contract.

If it's fraud, then there is no meeting of the minds, because one party has misrepresented a material fact to the other party. You can't have a meeting of the minds when one party misleads another as to a vital part of their agreement.

Why didn't the reporters simply disclose to me that they knew about Johnson's record at the time I showed them the documents?

Because they did not want me to know that they suspected Johnson had a record and they had not disclosed it to their readers.

Every Republican who ever lived believes the press follows a double standard, suppressing bad news about Democrats while broadcasting anything they can lay their hands on about Republicans.

So Sturdevant, who would not, could not, lie, because it was contrary to everything that is Lori Sturdevant, said nothing, and simply suggested I stop by again "any time I have material like this." Perhaps it was the best she could do, without lying or outright concealment.

And Salisbury, no more a liar than Sturdevant, but slightly more given to dramatics, said, "This is political dynamite."

Fraud, but no contract? I won, but was it for the wrong reasons?

I'll probably never know for sure. Salisbury wrote an article for the *Washington Journalism Review* in which he describes the incident just as he testified—that he hadn't been aware of Johnson's arrests. Apart from Sturdevant's sworn testimony, she has never commented or given an interview about the matter.

Maybe the reason the papers' lawyers conceded from the outset that the reporters had made me a promise was that they wanted us to focus on the contract claim. The papers could stand losing a breach of contract case, but they could not tolerate being publicly labeled as frauds. Allowing that kind of judgment would rip the heart out of their professional credibility.

So they could have decided to give us the easy score, the contract, knowing that no matter what happened at the trial level, no appellate court would sustain both a claim of a breach of contract and a fraud claim. Which is exactly what happened. When the case reached the Minnesota Court of Appeals, our fraud claim vanished. When we tried to revive it in the Minnesota Supreme Court, Justice Yetka realized what had happened, even though we didn't, and treated the facts as giving rise to promissory estoppel. This is the doctrine that even though our deal wasn't a contract, and even though we hadn't asked Sturdevant and Salisbury if they had known about Johnson's record and therefore couldn't establish fraud, we should still recover because we had reasonably relied on the promise given us by the reporters, and therefore, to be equitable, the law should recognize our claim. The phrase *promissory estoppel* means that defendants are, because of their behavior, estopped from asserting that we didn't have a true contract.

I suspect that days before I made my fateful journey to the bowels of the capitol, that either independently or through their reporters, the editors, too, had known that the first woman to run for lieutenant governor in the history of the state had a minor police record, and may have been a bit flaky in the bargain. Not too serious.

What was serious is if they had chosen not to inform their readers about it, and that I, through my bumbling, had made it so generally known, that they were forced to print it or be accused of suppressing it to benefit the Democratic ticket.

If I'd given the documents to only one paper, or even had I given it to both papers, but handled it furtively, correctly, in good 007 order, they could have simply ignored it. No one else would have known that they knew what I knew.

But once the *Star Tribune* knew that the *Pioneer Press* had it, and the *Pioneer Press* knew that the *Star Tribune* had it, the competitive pressures became overwhelming.

By virtue of my own stupidity and clumsiness, I was manipulating them. I was determining what they would print in their papers. I was making editorial decisions on the eve of a statewide election for the two largest newspapers in the state.

No wonder they were so pissed at me.

And when newspapers get that mightily annoyed, they know just how to express their displeasure. And they did. They burned me.

What's the meaning of it all?

So far as the *Star Tribune* and the *Pioneer Press* are concerned, it's business as usual. Though the papers were embarrassed nationally, locally they continue to operate like feudal lords, immune from any laws or standards, indifferent to the rights of others, duplicitous, biased, unfair, and often, just downright silly. True to form, neither paper ever did a story disclosing that they had once offered to pay me to pretend I had never received any money from them. As always, the people's right to know ends at their doorstep.

On August 21, 1995, the *New York Times* ran a feature article titled "Press Fad, or Future, in Minneapolis?," calling the *Star Tribune* "perhaps the most widely ridiculed newspaper in the country, described by critics inside the paper and out as a headquarters of political correctness and New Age journalism jargon." Now and forever, ridiculously liberal, even by the standards of the *New York Times*. The *Star Tribune* wears insults like that as a badge of honor. They once ran a classically nutty editorial, "Hear the Message of Political Correctness," defending the movement as akin to civil rights or feminism.

All the left-wing gibberish is just a disguise for the real life force around here: the lemming-like drive for conformity and its joined-at-the-hip twin, mediocrity.

Still, so far as I'm concerned personally, the case turned out better than I deserved. Of all life's blessings—health, wealth, and the rest—the rarest and sweetest is revenge. I got that—and more—the chance to replay Edwards, my most shameful public experience, and rewrite the ending. My goal was to redeem my honor. I wanted more. An acknowledgment from the papers that they had lied to me. An apology. A changing of the guard at the papers. I didn't get that. But I got enough, enough to get on with my life.

Epilogue

Rothenberg is still a sole practitioner, working out of his home.

Jim Fitzmaurice died in 1994. A blood clot, loosened by the chemotherapy he was receiving for lung cancer, blocked an artery and he collapsed and died of a heart attack in his driveway.

Paul Hannah continues to practice law in St. Paul.

Gary Flakne continues to practice law in the Minneapolis suburbs. He is still active in Republican politics.

Marlene Johnson served two terms as lieutenant governor. She married a Swedish businessman and divides her time between Minnesota and Sweden. When Rudy Perpich unsuccessfully ran for reelection as governor in 1990, he selected another running mate. Perpich died of colon cancer in 1995.

Wheelock Whitney was a key member of former Governor Arne Carlson's kitchen cabinet, and a part owner of the Minnesota Vikings. He also owns, breeds, and races thoroughbred horses.

Tim McGuire retired as editor of the *Star Tribune*. He writes a syndicated column that features mostly folksy, feel-good stories.

Lori Sturdevant has left the news side of the paper and is now an editorial writer for the *Star Tribune*.

Ron Edwards has had a remarkable career, becoming a one-man political force long after most of the people described here had vanished from the scene. After leaving the gas utility, Edwards spent the next twenty years in white-collar work at Northern States Power. He wrote a book, *The Minneapolis Story,* and currently has a weekly column in a black community newspaper.

John Cowles Jr. was ousted as President and CEO of Cowles Media in 1983. He and his wife, Sage, operate an interpretive dance studio.

Cowles Communications, the parent company of the *Minneapolis Star Tribune*, was acquired by McClatchy Newspapers for $1.4 billion in 1997. According to the *Star Tribune*, "it is believed to be the biggest price ever paid for a company whose primary asset is a newspaper." The sale transfers ownership of the third-largest independent from family ownership—John Cowles Sr. purchased the paper in 1935—to a chain.

Arnold Ismach, whose courage in testifying on my behalf made a significant contribution to the outcome of the case, has recently retired as dean of the Department of Journalism and Communication at the University of Oregon. He writes me that "since the trial, when I broke that unwritten rule [that you *never* testify against a newspaper] I've had only one consulting client [the company of a friend]. Before the trial, I did quite a bit of media consulting. Obviously, I was blacklisted for committing a cardinal sin."

This being Minnesota, most of the rest of the people mentioned in this book are now doing pretty much what they were doing at the time of the trial.

Let me close by apologizing to Marlene Johnson. Providing that stale, trivial record to the press was stupid and mean-spirited. I regret what I did.

Index